Pre-Intermediate

Matters

JAN BELL
ROGER GOWER

LONGMAN

Contents chart

Grammar	Vocabulary	Dictation and Pronunciation (See Workbook)
Question forms with the Present Simple, *be* and *have got* Question words Short answers	Countries, nationalities and languages	Dates and times Word stress
Present Continuous and Present Simple Adverbs of frequency	Buying clothes	Sound and spelling: /ə/ Clothes
Past Simple and Past Continuous	Personality types	Weak and contracted forms Giving personal information
Modals: obligation (*don't*) *have to*, *should(n't)*, *must(n't)*; possibility *can('t)*	At the doctor's	Sound and spelling: /iː/
The future: plans, decisions and arrangements (*will, going to* and the Present Continuous)	Transport	Pronunciation: /ðeə/ *they're, their, there*
Quantity expressions: *a, some, any, a few, a little, a lot, much, many*	Food and drink	Sound and spelling: /ɔː/ Contractions and weak forms
Present Perfect Simple or Past Simple? Time expressions: *just, ever, never, yet*	Feelings and opinions (*-ing* and *-ed* adjectives)	Questions and pronunciation
Verbs followed by *-ing* or *to*	Jobs	Sound and spelling: *o* An application form: names, dates, numbers and countries
Opinions: *will, won't, might, may* First Conditional	Rooms and furniture	Word stress Contracted forms
REVISION Question forms Obligation Mixed verb forms Quantity	REVISION Non-idiomatic phrasal verbs Idiomatic phrasal verbs	Sound and spelling: *c*
Comparative and superlative adjectives *as … as*	Hobbies	Spelling and the alphabet
Second Conditional	Crime	Grammar and pronunciation Sound and spelling: /v/ and /w/

INTRODUCTION *To the teacher*

These are some notes to help you before you begin.
The Students' Book contains twenty units, each divided into six sections: Use your English, Skills, Grammar, Vocabulary, Use and review and Language reference. This is how each unit is organised.

Use your English
This section revises and extends everyday English, including useful phrases and vocabulary. The aim is to develop students' confidence in being able to communicate.

Skills
In this section students will meet natural written and spoken English and develop techniques, such as deducing new words from context, using dictionaries and so on. Vocabulary areas are extended out of the text and practised.

Controlled Writing exercises help with organisational skills (the use of linking expressions, paragraph construction etc.). Specific linguistic areas which are necessary in writing (articles, adverbs etc.) are also presented and practised.

Grammar
There is oral and written controlled practice in each unit and at the end of the unit there is the Language reference section for study. The *Using your grammar* section in each unit gives communicative oppportunities to practise the grammar presented in a less controlled way.

Grammar	Vocabulary	Dictation and Pronunciation (See Workbook)
Defining relative clauses: *who, which, that, where* Adjective word order *We use a ... for ...-ing*	Describing people Relationships	Rhyming words Vocabulary
Used to Question tags	Entertainment	Sound and spelling: *a*
Quantity words: *some-, any-, no-, every-* *too* and *very* *too much* and *too many*	Education	Vocabulary and word stress
The passive (Present and Past Simple)	News stories	The passive
The unfinished past: Present Perfect Continuous and Present Perfect Simple *For* and *since*	Having a party	Contrastive stress
Sentence patterns (1): verb + person + *to* + base form of the verb Sentence patterns (2): reported sentences *say* and *tell*	Doing things in the house *Do* or *make ?*	Sentence completion Sound and spelling: *u*
Verb patterns (1): *if, when, as soon as, unless* Verb patterns (2): verb and 2 objects (*Give it to him. Give him the present.*)	Sports	Rhythm and sentence stress
REVISION Mixed practice Second Conditional Making comparisons Question tags	REVISION Phrasal verbs Mixed words	Sound and spelling: *g*

Word list PAGE 133   Tapescripts PAGE 137

Vocabulary
The Vocabulary section is mainly linked to the topic of the unit and includes a *Using your vocabulary* section to activate it.

Use and review
In this section there are communicative activities which revise the grammar and vocabulary presented in the preceding units. The exceptions to this pattern are Units 10 and 20 which revise the first and second half of the book respectively.

Language reference
The Language reference section provides a concise summary of the language covered in each unit.

Flexibility
Pre-Intermediate Matters Students' Book can be adapted to suit different teaching programmes. It can be extended by drawing on the extra practice in the Workbook, and activities and ideas in the Teacher's Book. For short courses, certain sections can be omitted. The sections within each unit of the Students' Book have been clearly signposted throughout to enable you to do this.

We hope you will enjoy the course and look forward to hearing how you get on.

Jan Bell and Roger Gower

•Do you remember me?•

USE YOUR ENGLISH

Starting a conversation

1 Look at the pictures from old films. The people are meeting for the first time.

a) What do you think they are saying?
b) [🖵 1.1] Listen. Match the pictures with the conversations.
c) Complete these sentences.

1 A: _____, is _____ free?   B: No, I'm sorry _____.
2 A: _____ somewhere before?   B: No, I'm afraid _____.
3 A: Would you like _____?   B: Yes, I'd _____.

d) Listen again and check your answers.
e) How do these people:

1 say *no* politely? (two ways)   3 say *yes* to an invitation?
2 invite someone to do something?

2 Here are some more ways of starting a conversation.

a) Match the expressions in A with the answers in B.

A	B
1 How are you?	a) Thanks.
2 It's a lovely day, isn't it?	b) Fine thanks.
3 Sorry I'm late.	c) How do you do?
4 Excuse me.	d) It doesn't matter.
5 Have a seat.	e) Yes? Can I help you?
6 Peter, this is Jack Smith.	f) Yes, beautiful.

b) [🖵 1.2] Listen and check your answers.
c) Work with a partner. Practise the ways of starting a conversation in Exercise 2a).
d) Go to someone in the class and start a conversation. Use some of the expressions in Exercises 1 and 2.

3 What do you do in your country?

a) What do you do when you meet someone?
b) Which of these questions is it impolite to ask when you do not know somebody very well?

1 How much do you earn?   4 Have you got any children?
2 What do you do?   5 How old are you?
3 Are you married?   6 Where do you live?

Amazing memories

A Dominic O'Brien, the World Memory Champion, is always a big success when he goes to a party. He can remember the names of more than a hundred people in only fifteen minutes! People can't believe it. And there is a man in China who can remember more than 15,000 telephone numbers! How do they do it? Most of us can't remember more than a few names or phone numbers.

How to remember...

B O'Brien believes that to improve your memory, you must exercise your brain as well as your body. Elderly people often lose their memories because they don't use their brains enough. He gives this advice for remembering names. When you meet someone new:

1 Think about who the person looks like. Imagine the person in a particular place. If he reminds you of a famous footballer, imagine him in goal.
2 When you learn the person's name, think of someone who has the same name. If the name is Ben and your dog's name is Ben, imagine your dog in goal!

The most important thing is to connect new information with places and ideas that you already know. This gives you a picture in your head which helps you to remember. We all remember the shape of Italy because it looks like a boot. But how can we remember the shape of Spain?

...and how to forget

C Perhaps a famous Russian had the most amazing memory of all. He could remember lists of hundreds of words and repeat them many years later. But he had a big problem – it was difficult for him to forget information. He had to imagine the information on a board. Then he could rub it out in his head. That was the only way he could forget.

SKILLS

Reading and speaking

1   How good is your memory?

a) Do you ever forget things? What?

b) What do you do to help you remember?

2   Read the newspaper article on the left.

a) Match the pictures and the paragraphs.

b) The writer of the article talks about the best way to improve your memory. What does he say? Do you agree?

c) Are these sentences *True* (T) or *False* (F)?

1 Old people often lose their memories because they don't take exercise.
2 When you meet a person, always imagine him in goal on a football field.
3 It is easier to remember the shape of some countries than others.
4 It is important to connect the name of the person you are meeting with someone or something you know.
5 The Russian could never forget anything.

Vocabulary

1   Look at the underlined words. What part of speech are they? Are they verbs, adverbs, adjectives or nouns?
Elderly people *often* *lose* their *memories*.

> groups and black berries (elderberries)
> **elderly** / ˈeldəlɪ / *adj (of a person)*
> getting near old age
> **elder statesman** *n* an old and respected

2   Look at the dictionary extract.
a) What part of speech is *elderly*? How do you know?
b) Find four new words in the article. What part of speech are the words? Use a dictionary to help you.

3   The dictionary also gives you the pronunciation of *elderly*.

a) Look at the phonemic chart on page 132. How do you pronounce /ə/? How do you pronounce /ɪ/?
b) Which is the stressed syllable in ˈ*elderly*? How do you know?

Writing: punctuation

a) In English we use a capital letter at the beginning of a sentence and a full stop at the end. We use a question mark if the sentence is a question. Examples:
This is a new sentence.
Is this a new sentence?

b) We also use capital letters for the names of particular things. Examples:
- people *(John)*
- places *(Oxford Street)*
- countries *(Switzerland)*
- nationalities *(Swiss)*
- languages *(French)*
- days and months *(Monday, January)*
- titles *(The Times)*

c) We use commas:
- to divide a sentence and make it easier to understand. Example: *The woman I was talking to, who lives next door, is very nice.*
- to divide things in a list. Example: *I eat fish, eggs, cheese and nuts.*

Rewrite the paragraphs below. Put in the correct punctuation. Both paragraphs should have three sentences.

1
dominic o'brien the memory man lives near cambridge when he is not trying to remember things he spends his time playing the piano gardening and cycling he eats a lot of bananas apples and oranges which help his brain

2
my family live in switzerland and we speak german from monday to friday I work in an office in the centre of geneva i live in the country with my parents two sisters my dog and rabbit

GRAMMAR

Questions and answers

1 Look at the pictures.

a) What questions are the people asking?

The verbs *be* and *have got*

When we form questions we put the auxiliary verb before the subject.

Be

POSITIVE	QUESTION	NEGATIVE
I am ...	*Am I ... ?*	*I'm (am) not ...*
You / We / They are ...	*Are you / we / they ... ?*	*You / We / They aren't (are not) ...*
He / She / It is ...	*Is he / she / it ...?*	*He / She / It isn't (is not) ...*

Have got

POSITIVE	QUESTION	NEGATIVE
I / You / We / They have got ...	*Have I / you / we / they got ... ?*	*I / You / We / They haven't (have not) got ...*
He / She / It has got ...	*Has he / she / it got ... ?*	*He / She / It hasn't (has not) got ...*

Other verbs: Present Simple

When we form questions with other verbs we put the auxiliary *do* or *does* before the subject. The base form of the verb follows.

POSITIVE	QUESTION	NEGATIVE
I like music.	*Do I like music?*	*I don't (do not) like music.*
You / We / They eat meat.	*Do you / we / they eat meat?*	*You / We / They don't (do not) eat meat.*
He / She / It walks slowly.	*Does he / she / it walk slowly?*	*He / She / It doesn't (does not) walk slowly.*

have / time?

an.

Yes, I have. It's nearly three o'clock.

b) [🎧 1.3]. Listen and check your answers to 1a).

> a) In questions the auxiliaries usually have weak pronunciation. Example:
> *Do you come here often?* / dju:kəmhɪənfən /
> b) The auxiliaries usually have the strong form in short answers. Example:
> *Yes, he does* or *Yes, I am*. But in the negative they have the weak or contracted form. Example: *No, I'm not*.
> c) In short answers we repeat the auxiliary from the question (*do/does, have, be, can*). Example: *Do you smoke? Yes, I do*. This is more polite than *Yes* or *No*.

2   Look at the grammar boxes opposite.

a) Make *Yes/No* questions for these sentences.
Example:
He lives in New York.
Does he live in New York?

1 We're going.
2 They drink a lot of coffee.
3 They're over there.
4 This seat is free.
5 They've got the tickets.
6 She's got a blue car.
7 I'm ready.
8 He can swim.
9 You know her.

b) Make two lists of the questions: 1 Questions with the auxiliary *do/does* ; 2 Other questions.
c) Now give short answers to the questions. The answers should be *Yes* for 1-5 and *No* for 6-9. Example:
A: *Are you going?*
B: *Yes, we are.*

Question words

These are the answers to some questions.

1 I'm an engineer.
2 At about midnight.
3 Because I need it for my job.
4 My favourite singer? Oh, Whitney Houston, I think.
5 The United States.
6 It's mine.
7 On foot.
8 Four.
9 That one over there.

a) Match the answers above with a question word from the box.

where	how	what
how many		which
why	when	who
whose		

b) Make questions to go with these answers. Example:
A: *What do you do?*
B: I'm an engineer.
c) [🎧 1.4] Listen and compare your answers.
d) Work with a partner. Practise asking and answering the questions.

Using your grammar

1   You are interviewing the actor Jay Shepherd for a magazine article.

a) Work with a partner. Write questions to ask him about:

age? married? single? engaged? family? children? nationality? Where / live? What / do / at the moment? What music, clothes etc. / like?

b) [🎧 1.5] Listen to an interview with Jay Shepherd. Make notes to answer your questions.
c) Find out about people in your class. Ask questions.
Example:
Where do you live?

VOCABULARY

Countries and nationalities

1   Work in groups. Answer these questions as quickly as you can.

a) These are the capital cities of which countries?

1 Brussels	3 Madrid	5 Lisbon	7 Amsterdam
2 Warsaw	4 Edinburgh	6 Ankara	8 Tokyo

b) In which country is:

1 The Great Wall?	3 The Parthenon?	5 The Vatican?
2 Mecca?	4 The White House?	6 Big Ben?

c) Which countries are the pictures on the right connected with?

d) What nationality is/was:

1 Picasso?	3 Charlie Chaplin?	5 Walt Disney?	7 Pelé?
2 Mozart?	4 Gandhi?	6 Tolstoy?	8 Napoleon?

e) What is the official language of :

1 Brazil?	3 Mexico?	5 the Netherlands?	7 Austria?
2 Jamaica?	4 Japan?	6 Corsica?	8 Egypt?

2   Make three lists of words from Exercise 1: 1 Countries; 2 Languages; and 3 Nationalities.

a) Add more countries, languages and nationalities.
b) Mark the stressed syllable in each word. Use a dictionary to help you. Example: *'Brussels.*
c) Practise the pronunciation and stress of the countries and nationalities. Remember that we often pronounce unstressed vowels as /ə/. Example: /brə'zɪl/.

Using your vocabulary

Work in small groups.

a) Write questions about countries, nationalities and languages. Examples:
Where is .....? What language do people in ..... speak? Is ..... in .....? What nationality is/was .....?
b) Use your dictionary to check the stress in each word. Then ask the class the questions.

USE AND REVIEW

1   Pronouns and possessive adjectives. How much do you remember?

ACROSS

1 Goodbye, madam. Here is _____ coat.
2 Give the ball to _____. We want to play with it.
5 A: Whose is this?   B: Ben and Joe are over there. Maybe it's _____.
7 A: Where's Jane?   B: _____'s over there.
8 A: Is it Anne's?   B: No, it's not _____.
9 Have you got a biscuit for _____? I'm hungry.

DOWN

3 The coat belongs to Susy. It's _____' coat.
4 A: Whose is the red car?   B: It's _____. I bought it last week.
5 Where are your friends? I can't see _____.
6 A: Is Tom here?   B: Yes, _____ is.
8 Give the pen to _____. It's his.

2   Work in groups. Talk about your experiences of learning languages.

a) What other languages have you learned? Did you enjoy the experience? Why/Why not?
b) Look at this list. Which are the most important for you? What do you enjoy most? Number them from 1-7. (1 = very important/very enjoyable 7 = not important/not enjoyable).

	important	enjoyable
vocabulary	_____	_____
grammar	_____	_____
pronunciation	_____	_____
reading	_____	_____
listening	_____	_____
speaking	_____	_____
writing	_____	_____

Language reference

1 Question forms

a) *be* and *have got*

We put the subject after the verb.

Verb	Subject	
Am	*I*	*late?*
Have	*you / we / they*	**got** *any change?*

In informal language British people usually use *have got* not *have* for possession. We can also use the auxiliary *do* or *does* with *have* for possession (NOT with *have got*) in the question form.
Does he **have** any children?

b) Modals

With modal verbs (*can, could, would* etc.) we also put the modal verb before the subject in questions.
He would like a drink. **Would he** *like a drink?*

c) Verbs in the Present Simple

We put the auxiliary *do/does* before the subject and the base form of the verb.

Auxiliary	Subject	Base form	
Do	*I / you / we / they*	**want**	*one?*
Does	*he / she / it*	**have**	*breakfast?*

d) Verbs in the Present Continuous

We put the auxiliary *be* before the subject. We add *-ing* to the base form of the verb.

Be	Subject	Base form + *-ing*	
Am	*I*	**working**	
Are	*we / they / you*	**eating**	*now?*
Is	*he / she / it*	**leaving?**	

2 Question words

We often put a question word before the auxiliary verb.

Question word	Auxiliary	Subject	Main Verb
What / which (cake)	*do*	*you*	*want?*
Where	*does*	*he*	*live?*
When	*is*	*he*	*going?*
How many	*has*	*he*	*got?*
Why	*are*	*they*	*leaving?*
Who	*is*	*he*	*talking to?*
Whose (pen)	*is*	*it?*	

An adjective or adverb often follows *how* (*tall, many* etc.), and a noun often follows *what/ which/ whose* (*cake, pen* etc.).

3 Short answers

(See page 9.)

•Spend, spend, spend!•

USE YOUR ENGLISH

Public places

1   Look at the pictures.

a) Where would you hear these requests? Match the sentences with the pictures.

  1 Have you got a small brown loaf, please?
  2 Can I have white, no sugar, please?
  3 Could I have ten first class stamps?
  4 May I change these traveller's cheques?

b) [🔲 2.1]   Listen and check your answers.
c) Which of the requests sounded more polite? Why?
d) Listen again. How did people ask other people to do things? Complete the sentences.

  1 _____ two white coffees, please?
  2 _____ sign here, please?

e) How did people answer the requests? Complete the sentences.

  1 _____, but we've only got white bread left.
  2 _____. Two white coffees, no sugar.
  3 _____, _____ are.
  4 _____. How would you like your money?

2   You need to buy the things on the shopping list.

a) Match the things on the list with the shops in the box.

> chemist's   jeweller's   butcher's
> greengrocer's   bookshop

Shopping list
Steven King's
  new novel
6 chicken legs
cough mixture
watch strap
potatoes
grapes

b) What other things can you buy from these shops? Make a list.

3   Work with a partner. Choose one of the places in Exercises 1 or 2. Write a short conversation. Use the requests and answers from Exercise 1. Example: At a jeweller's
CUSTOMER: *Excuse me.*
ASSISTANT: *Yes? Can I help you?*
CUSTOMER: *I'd like a new watch strap, please.*
ASSISTANT: *Yes, of course. What colour would you like?*

SKILLS

Listening and speaking

1 Read this newspaper article and answer the questions below.

When Japanese visitors to Britain go home they often take umbrellas, china or tea as souvenirs. But five Japanese businessmen have just paid half a million pounds for a traditional British cottage. They will rebuild it when they get back to Japan.
This is not a completely new idea. You can also find red telephone boxes and black taxi cabs in Japan. It seems that anything 'traditional' is popular there.

1 What souvenirs do Japanese people usually buy when they go to Britain?
2 What unusual souvenirs have some Japanese people taken home?
3 What do people buy when they come to your country?
4 Would you buy any of the souvenirs below? Why?/ Why not?

2 [2.2] Listen to Tanya and David. They are talking about how they spend their money. Answer these questions.

1 Which of these do they talk about?

holidays	computers	music	things for the house
clothes	jewellery	food	things for the garden
videos	sports	books	photography

2 Which of these things does Tanya spend her money on?
3 What does David spend his money on?
4 What do *you* spend your money on?

3 [2.3] Listen to the next part of the conversation and make notes about

1 three kinds of souvenir that Tanya brings back.
2 two kinds of souvenir that David brings back.
3 their bad experiences with souvenirs.

4 Work in groups. Tell each other about the best, the worst and the most expensive thing you have ever bought.

5 [2.4] Read and listen to four sentences from the interview with David and Tanya.

a) Listen to the pronunciation of *for, a, as, of* and *from*. We don't stress the vowels. The pronunciation is weak and the vowel sound is /ə/.

1 I don't spend anything for months.
2 I'm a student, as you know.
3 I've got about forty of them.
4 From all over the world.

b) Work with a partner. Read the sentences. Remember to use the weak pronunciation /ə/ where necessary.

Vocabulary

These are some of the things David and Tanya say. Use the sentences to guess the meanings of the words in italics.

1 I don't spend anything for months. I just *save* and *save*.
2 I love jewellery so ... I brought back a lot of *earrings* and big necklaces.
3 ... an *enormous* plant pot – so big I couldn't see over the top.
4 I *collect* T-shirts – I've got about forty of them from all over the world.

Writing: spelling rules

-ing and -s

> We form the Present Continuous by adding -ing to the base form of the verb. Example: *eat → eating*.
> We form the third person of the Present Simple by adding -s to the base form of the verb. Example: *eat → eats*.
> But there are some exceptions:
>
> **1 -ing**
>
> a) When the word ends in -e, drop the final -e *(take → taking)*.
> b) With one syllable words, double the final consonant if it ends with only one consonant *(hit → hitting)*. But if the word ends with two consonants, don't double the final consonant *(jump → jumping)*.
>
> **2 -s**
>
> a) add -es with *do* and *go* *(does; goes)*.
> b) add -es after words which end in -ch and -sh *(touch → touches; push → pushes)*.
> c) add -ies if the word ends in a consonant + -y *(marry → marries)*.

Correct this student's mistakes. There are two mistakes in each sentence. Match the mistakes with the rules in the box above.

1 James is siting in his room, drinking a cup of tea and writing a letter.
2 Flora is makeing a cake and putting some chocolate on it because her friend is comeing to tea.
3 She usually gos by train or bus but she never flys because she hates planes.
4 Tim enjoys television so he sometimes carrys the TV up to his bedroom and watchs it alone.

GRAMMAR

Talking about the present

Peter

> I don't usually wear clothes like these for work. But it's the first day of my new job so I want to look smart.

> I'm taking the dog for a walk so I need to be comfortable. But I really prefer smart clothes – skirts, jackets and so on.

Joy

Mary

> I'm going to a fancy dress party. That's why I'm wearing these clothes. I don't usually wear black. I like bright colours.

> I always wear casual clothes like these – sometimes a tracksuit. My boss says it's OK, as long as we're clean and tidy.

Alison

1 Look at the photographs.

a) Find an example of the Present Simple and the Present Continuous.

b) Which form of the verb do we use when:

1 we talk about what we *often* or *usually* do?
2 we talk about what we are doing *now*?

c) Look at the grammar boxes at the top of page 15 and complete these sentences with the correct form of the verb *wear*.

1 I usually _____ jeans or long skirts but at the moment I _____ fancy dress.
2 He doesn't usually _____ formal clothes for work but he _____ a suit today.

Present Simple

POSITIVE

Subject	Verb	
I/You/We/They	**speak**	English.
He/She	**speaks**	

NEGATIVE

Subject	Negative	Base form	
I/You/We/They	**don't (do not)**	**speak**	English.
He/She	**doesn't (does not)**		

Present Continuous

POSITIVE

Subject + be	Base form + -ing	
I'm (am)		
You/We/They**'re (are)**	**speaking**	English.
He/She**'s (is)**		

NEGATIVE

Subject + be	Base form + -ing	
I'm not (am not)		
You/We/They **aren't (are not)**	**speaking**	English.
He/She **isn't (is not)**		

2   Look at the people in the photos again.

a) What are they wearing? Use the words in the box. Example:
Peter is wearing a suit.

sweatshirt	trainers	boots
leggings	pointed hat	tie
suit	jeans	jumper	dress

b) Do they usually wear clothes like these? If not, why are they wearing them now?

3   Complete these sentences. Use the Present Simple or the Present Continuous.

1 Helen *(walk)* _____ to work nearly every day but today she *(go)* _____ by car.
2 A: Where's Clare?
   B: She *(put)* _____ the baby to bed.
3 A: Where *(Josh / live)* _____?
   B: In Canada, I think. But he *(stay)* _____ with Brenda in Scotland this month.
4 It never *(snow)* _____ in July. But today it *(rain)* _____ very heavily.
5 A: What *(you / do)* _____ now?
   B: I *(clean)* _____ the windows.

Adverbs of frequency

Princess Diana is often in the public eye but she's usually nervous in front of a lot of people. In this picture she is playing with her ring. Psychologist Jane Carman says nervous habits like this can sometimes tell us how people are feeling.

> Adverbs of frequency like *sometimes, usually* or *never* come before main verbs but after auxiliary verbs like *be, have* and *do/does.*

a) Work with a partner. Find examples of frequency adverbs above.
b) What other nervous habits do you sometimes have? Example: *biting your lip.*
c) Write down one thing that you *always, never, sometimes* and *often* do. Ask your partner about what he/she *often* and *never* wears.

Using your grammar

What's wrong with the picture? Write down as many things as you can. Example:
A woman is taking a cat for a walk.

a) Work with a partner. Check each other's spelling. (Remember the rules on page 14.)
b) Look at the picture again and practise the contracted form of the Present Continuous. Example:
She's taking a cat for a walk.
c) What do people usually do? Example:
***They don't take** cats for a walk. **They take** dogs.*

VOCABULARY

Buying clothes

Look at the clothes in the picture.

a) Do you know the English words for these clothes? Make a list of as many words as you can.

b) [📼 2.5] Listen to the conversation in a clothes shop. When you hear a word on your list, tick (✓) it .

c) Listen again and complete these sentences.

1 Is this jumper _____?
2 Could I _____ in _____?
3 What _____ are you?
4 The _____ rooms are _____.

5 Does it _____?
6 _____ a 10?
7 No, I'm sorry we've _____.

d) Write the words in your vocabulary book. Mark the stressed syllable in each word. Use a dictionary to help you. Example: *py'jamas*.

Using your vocabulary

1   What type and colour of clothes do you usually buy? What do you never buy? What would you buy if money was no problem?

2   Imagine that someone has stolen all your clothes. You have enough money to buy only twelve items of clothing. Make a list of the clothes you would buy and the colours.

Work in groups. Compare your lists.

USE AND REVIEW

1   Work with a partner.

> **STUDENT A**
> Read the article about Thomas Webber. Imagine you are him. Complete the article with 'facts' about yourself.

> **STUDENT B**
> Read the article about Joanne Young. Imagine you are her. Complete the article with 'facts' about yourself.

THOMAS WEBBER is _____ years old and lives in _____. He is married with _____ young children. He is a very famous musician. He plays the _____ in an orchestra in Liverpool and often appears on TV. At the moment Thomas is working in _____. Mozart is his favourite composer, but he loves _____, too.

JOANNE YOUNG is well-known as a _____. She is engaged to a man called _____, who is a _____. Joanne lives in the United States but she is _____. However, she speaks English perfectly. She hasn't got any children, but she has three pets – a _____, a _____ and a _____. In her spare time she likes _____ and _____.

a) Look at the other article. Some of the information is missing. What questions can you ask to get the information? Example: *How old are you?*

b) Interview your partner. Find out the missing information.

c) Complete the article about the person you interviewed.

2   Find someone in the class who knows the answers to all these questions.

1 Where is a) Ankara   b) the Great Wall?
2 What nationality is/was a) Pelé   b) Mozart?
3 What official language do people speak in:
  a) the Netherlands   b) Corsica   c) Brazil?
4 Where do koala bears come from?
5 Which country is the Eiffel Tower in?

Language reference

1 Present Simple

FORM
(See pages 11, 14 and 15.)

USE
We use the Present Simple to talk about:
a) something which we often or usually do (a routine):
  *He **goes** to work at eight o'clock every day.*
b) a situation in the present which is true (a state):
  *I **live** in Mexico.*
c) something which is always true (a fact):
  *It **gets** dark at night.*

2 Adverbs of frequency

Words like *always, never* etc. describe how often you do something.

never	rarely	sometimes	often	usually	always
0%					100%

3 Present Continuous

FORM
(See page 15.)

USE
We use the Present Continuous to talk about something temporary which is happening:
a) at the moment of speaking
  *'Where's Jim?' 'He**'s watching** TV.'*
b) around the time of speaking (but not at that exact moment)
  *You look tired. You**'re working** too hard.*

We also use it to talk about planned arrangements in the future (See Unit 5, page 35).

•The family unit•

USE YOUR ENGLISH

Talking about families

1   This is a photo of Lucy and her family on her wedding day.

a) Who do you think the people are? Who are Lucy's parents? Who are her grandparents, sister, brother, brother-in-law, nephew, niece, uncle, aunts, cousins? Give your reasons. Example:
I think Max is her brother, because he looks like her.

b) What do you think of the people? How old are they? Use some of the expressions in the box. Example:
Max looks interesting. I think he's in his twenties.

interesting   attractive quite/very young around/about twenty middle-aged   nice in his/her teens/forties

2 [▭ 3.1]   Listen to Lucy talking about her relations.

a) Now say who the people are in the photograph. Example:
Sam is her cousin.

b) Listen again and complete these sentences.

1 Lucy's _____ are divorced.
2 Lucy's stepfather is called _____.
3 Lucy's older brother is working in _____. He's an _____.
4 _____ is engaged.
5 _____ is Australian.
6 _____ are twenty-five.

3   Work with a partner.

a) Ask questions about his/her family. Example:
Have you got any brothers or sisters? How old are they? Where do they live?

b) Draw a family tree of your partner's family. Look at the example on the right.

c) Check with your partner that his/her family tree is correct.

d) Work in groups. Talk about your partner's family.

Flora = Gianni
|
Marisa = Claudio
|
Sergio   Antonio

SKILLS

Speaking and reading

1 Look at the photo of Kate Moss, and her younger brother, Nick. They are models.

a) Do you think Kate looks like Nick?

b) Do you take after anyone in your family? Who? In what way? Example:
I look like my father but I have my mother's personality.

c) Is there anyone you get on well with? Example:
I'm very close to my younger sister.

d) Is there anyone you don't get on with? Example:
I don't like my cousin.

he couldn't remember his first words.
get on with sbdy. *phr v* (of people)
to have a friendly relationship
get on for sthg. *phr v* [L+n; in progressive forms] *esp. BrE* to be almost reaching
when you die ■ phrasal verbs.
take after sbdy *phr v*
to look or behave like an older relative
take apart *phr v* [T] 1 (take sthg.
←→apart) to separate (a small machine,

2 Before you read the newspaper article guess the answers to these questions.

1 Are Kate and Nick interested in clothes?
2 How did Kate first become a model?
3 Is modelling very different for men and women?

3 Read the article.

a) Were your guesses correct?

b) Are these sentences *True* (T) or *False* (F)?

1 Kate and Nick have different personalities.
2 Their parents work in the fashion business.
3 Kate always wanted to be a model.
4 Kate and Nick had lots of fights when they were young.
5 Nick doesn't see his mother very often.
6 Nick and his father have a good relationship.
7 Nick does not want to be a model all his life.

4 Some of the words in the article have a short /ɪ/ sound. Example: *sister*.

a) Practise saying these words: str**i**ct, r**i**p, b**i**t, s**i**lly.

b) The /ɪ/ sound sometimes has other spellings. Practise saying these words: b**ui**ld, d**e**cided, b**u**sy, b**e**gin, w**o**men, **E**ngl**i**sh.

c) [▣ 3.2] Listen and check your pronunciation.

Me and my family

BY   NICK   MOSS

My sister takes after my mum, but people say I take after my dad. He's a travel consultant and he's
5 got his own business. He's always nice and friendly.

My mother shows her feelings more. She works as a barmaid in a wine bar and she's quite attractive. She's got dark hair
10 and a nice face with dark brown eyes.

Kate is funny and a bit different. She changes the way she dresses every week. I am not very interested in fashion – I like my jeans and old clothes.
15 Kate lives and works in a lot of different countries. I stayed with her in New York when we were doing a job together. We went shopping and everyone knew her because there were
20 posters of her everywhere.

Somebody from a model agency saw Kate at JFK airport in New York when she was 14 or 15. We were coming back from a holiday in Florida with dad and a
25 woman said, 'Do you want to come down to the model agency?' Kate had never thought about modelling before that – she was just a normal girl then.

When we were young we had fights
30 about silly little things. It was fantastic! She sometimes hit me so I ripped up her posters and threw her clothes on the floor.

My parents are divorced but they get
35 on quite well. I live with my dad but my mum lives very near and I see her about three times a week. I get on brilliantly with my dad – we can talk about everything. He's very easygoing and not
40 strict, but he keeps me under control.

Kate loves modelling. If you are a woman you can earn a lot of money, but the job is not so good for men. I enjoy modelling, but I would prefer to play
45 football professionally or manage a hotel. I suppose I'm quite ambitious – I want to succeed.

(from *The Daily Telegraph*)

Vocabulary: adjectives

Adjectives often have one of these endings: *-al, -ive, -ent, -y, -ous, -ic, -ly*.

Find an adjective in the article on page 19 which means:

1 kind, ready to help (line 6)
2 good looking (line 9)
3 someone/thing that makes you laugh (line 11)
4 not the same, unusual (line 11)
5 like everyone else (line 28)
6 really good (line 30)
7 someone who wants to get a very good job and earn a lot of money (line 46)

Writing: linking words

a) **and** = more information.
   *Kate's father is friendly **and** easy-going.*
b) **but** = more information which doesn't follow.
   *Nick is a model **but** he's not interested in clothes.*
c) **because** = reason.
   *Kate became a model **because** someone saw her at·an airport.*
d) **so** = result.
   *Kate hit Nick **so** Nick threw her clothes on the floor.*

Join these sentences to make one sentence. Use one of the linking words above.

1 He failed his exam. He couldn't go to university.
2 Last year I went to France. I went to Turkey.
3 I saw the car coming towards me. I couldn't stop.
4 I left the beach early. I was very hot.

GRAMMAR

Past Simple and Past Continuous

Past Simple

Look at the pictures on the right. These things happened yesterday morning before Liz went to work.

a) Work with a partner. What order did they happen in?
Example: 1 = *f*

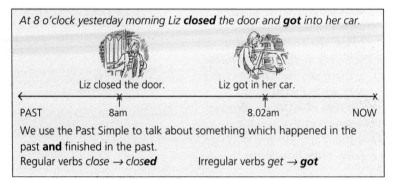

At 8 o'clock yesterday morning Liz **closed** the door and **got** into her car.

Liz closed the door.   Liz got in her car.

PAST   8am   8.02am   NOW

We use the Past Simple to talk about something which happened in the past **and** finished in the past.
Regular verbs *close → closed*   Irregular verbs *get → got*

b) Look at the pictures again. What happened yesterday morning? Use the verbs in the box. Example:
The alarm clock rang at 7 o'clock.

ring get up make read eat wash up have take

c) What is the Past Simple of these verbs: walk, begin, do, decide, drink, fall, sell, sit, leave, teach, write, sing, feel, put, go, hear, play, wake?

Questions and answers

Liz got up at 7 o'clock.

Did Liz get up at 8 o'clock? No, she didn't.

She went downstairs.

Did Liz go downstairs? Yes, she did.

Work with a partner.

a) Ask and answer questions about Liz. Use the Past Simple and short answers. Example: Liz / go / for a walk / with her baby?
A: *Did Liz go for a walk with her baby?*
B: *No, she didn't. She went for a walk with her dog.*

1 Liz / have / a bath?
2 she / wash / her clothes?
3 she / have / a cup of tea for breakfast?
4 Liz / watch / the television?

b) Ask your partner questions about yesterday morning. Example:
Did you have breakfast?

Past Continuous

*Liz **was reading** the newspaper when the postman arrived.*

The postman arrived.

PAST   Liz **was reading** the newspaper.   NOW

1   Look at the timeline.

a) Did Liz begin reading the newspaper before the postman arrived?

b) Which is the short completed action? Which is the longer activity?

c) What do you think Liz did when the postman arrived?

2 [▭ 3.3]   Listen to these sounds in Liz's house yesterday.

a) What was happening?

b) Which were the longer actions? Which actions interrupted them?

c) Listen again. Complete these sentences.

1 When Liz _____ it _____ outside and the birds _____.
2 While Liz _____ a shower the phone _____.
3 She _____ a plate when she _____.

d) [▭ 3.4]   Listen and check your answers.

3   Change the verbs in brackets to the Past Simple or the Past Continuous.

Liz *(wake up)* (1) _____ at 7 o'clock. She *(get up)* (2) _____, *(put on)* (3) _____ her dressing gown and *(go)* (4) _____ downstairs. She *(make)* (5) _____ some toast and some coffee. The phone *(ring)* (6) _____ while she *(have)* (7) _____ a shower, but she *(not answer)* (8) _____ it. After her shower she *(get dressed)* (9) _____ and *(take)* (10) _____ the dog for a walk in the park. At eight o'clock she *(leave)* (11) _____ the house to go to work. But as she *(drive)* (12) _____ down the motorway, she *(turn on)* (13) _____ the radio and *(hear)* (14) _____ the newsreader say, 'Good morning. I hope you are all enjoying a relaxing Bank Holiday Monday!'

[▭ 3.5]   Listen and check your answers.

Using your grammar

Work with a partner. Talk about:

1 your first day at school
2 your first love
3 the first thing you remember buying
4 your first time away from home
5 the first news story you remember

VOCABULARY

Personality types

1 Professor Max Schmidt is a psychologist. He believes that people's favourite colours tell us a lot about their personalities.

a) Look at the colours. Which is your favourite?

b) Match the adjectives in italics with their meanings. Example:
1 = *independent*

1 you don't need other people
2 you don't think before doing something
3 young for your age
4 full of life and energy
5 you like spending money
6 very relaxed, not in a hurry

c) What does your favourite colour say about your personality? Do you agree?

2 Look at the adjectives in the box.

> good-tempered   fun   honest   patient   generous   affectionate

a) Match the adjectives with their meanings. Somebody who ...

1 doesn't tell lies is _____.
2 spends money on other people is _____.
3 is rarely angry is _____.
4 is calm and happy to wait is _____.
5 you can have a good time with is _____.
6 shows they like you is _____.

b) [3.6] Listen to Tom and Diana talking about their families. Who talks about his/her cat, Grandad, Mum, Dad?

c) Listen again and complete these sentences with adjectives from the box above.

1 My Grandad is _____.
2 My Mum is _____.
3 My cat is _____.
4 My Dad is _____.

Using your vocabulary

1 Which qualities do you think are important in these people? Example:
I think it's important for a friend to be honest.

- friend
- boss
- wife/husband
- boyfriend/girlfriend
- parent
- grandparent

2 Write a short poem about someone you like very much. Start each line with a letter of their first name. Give the poem a title. Look at the example on the right.

Personality types

● You are *extravagant*. You like a good life.

● You are a bit *immature*. You seem younger than other people.

● You are quite *independent* and like being alone.

● This suggests that you are *lively* and *energetic*.

● This means that you are *easygoing* and calm.

● This can show that you are sometimes *thoughtless*.

A good friend

Generous
Interesting
Laughs a lot
Likes having fun
GILL!

USE AND REVIEW

1   Work with a partner.

STUDENT A
Look at page 126.

STUDENT B

a) You are a customer in a clothes shop. Look at your rolecard and think about what you are going to say.

> ROLECARD
>
> You are going somewhere (on holiday? to an important meeting?) and you need new clothes. Think about these questions: Where are you going? How much can you spend? What do you want to buy? What colours, sizes and styles do you like? Go to the shop and ask the shop assistant to help you. (*Could I ...? Would you ...?*) Ask to try things on. Ask about prices and how to pay – credit card, cheque or cash?

b) Have a conversation with your partner.

2   Work with a partner.

STUDENT A
Look at page 126.

STUDENT B
Look at this picture. You and your partner have similar pictures but there are some differences. Take turns to talk about your picture. When you find a difference you should both write it down. Example:
A: *In my picture the baby is crying.*
B: *In my picture the baby is sleeping.*

Now find five more differences.

Language reference

1 Past Simple

USE
We use the Past Simple to talk about something which happened in the past and is now finished.

FORM
Base form of the verb + *-ed*. See page 132 for irregular verbs.

Positive
*I / You / We / They / He / She / It **arrived** late.*
Negative
*We **didn't arrive** late.*
Questions
*When **did** I / you we / they / he / she / it **arrive**?*
Short answers
*Did he go to the party?   Yes, he **did**. / No, he **didn't**.*

2 Past Continuous

FORM

Past of *be* + base form of the verb + *-ing*.

Positive
*I / He / She **was watching** television at 9 o'clock.* *You / We / They **were having** lunch when he arrived.*
Negative
*I / He / She **wasn't (was not) listening** to him.* *You / We / They **weren't (were not) watching** the film.*
Questions
***Was** I / he / she **driving** fast?* ***Were** we / they **talking** to him?*
Short answers
*Were you listening?   Yes, I **was.** / No, I **wasn't**.*

USE

a) We use the Past Continuous to talk about something that was already happening at a particular time in the past.
   *What **were** you **doing** at half past eight?*
   Compare this with the Past Simple for a shorter action.
   *What **did** you **do** at half past eight?*
b) To talk about longer 'background' actions which are 'interrupted' by shorter actions.
   *The children **were fighting** when their mother **arrived.***
   Compare this with two short actions one after the other.
   *When their mother **came in** the children **ran** to her.*
c) To describe people, places etc.
   *She **was wearing** jeans and a shirt.*

•Me and my body•

USE YOUR ENGLISH

On the phone

1   Today is Monday, 15 August.

a) Work with a partner. Look at Emma's plans for the next two
weeks. When is she doing these things? Example:
going to the hairdresser's
*She's going to the hairdresser's tomorrow, 16 August, at twenty
past eleven.*

   1 seeing her bank manager   3 having lunch with her aunt
   2 going to the cinema   4 babysitting for Tina

b) How do we say dates? How do we write them?

2   Emma made three phone calls this morning.

a) [📼 4.1]   Listen and complete her diary.
b) Emma talks to four people. Which of the people does not
sound friendly?

3 [📼 4.2]   Listen to parts of the first conversation again.
Complete these sentences.

   1 EMMA: Hello. _____ a table free on _____, please,
           at _____?
   2 MAN: _____ just _____.
   3 MAN: _____ take your name, please?
     EMMA: Yes, it's _____.
   4 MAN: And _____ have your phone number?
     EMMA: _____. It's _____.

4 [📼 4.3]   Listen to the second conversation again and
answer these questions.

   1 What does Carol say when she answers the phone? What do
     you say in *your* country?
   2 What does Emma say next?
   3 Carol asks Emma to wait. What does she say? What is a more
     formal way of saying this?
   4 Emma invites Simon to play tennis. What does she say?
   5 How does she offer to book the tennis court?

5   Work with a partner.

STUDENT A: Look at page 126.
STUDENT B: Look at page 128.

Monday 15	3 p.m. Take car to garage
Tuesday 16	11.20 Hairdresser's
Wednesday 17	10.30 See bank manager
Thursday 18	a.m. Cat to vet's
Friday 19	
Saturday 20	(evening) Cinema
Sunday 21	12.30 Lunch with Auntie Sally
Monday 22	8 p.m. Babysit for Tina
Tuesday 23	
Wednesday 24	
Thursday 25	
Friday 26	
Saturday 27	

SKILLS

Reading and speaking

1 When people want to be healthy they sometimes do these things.

a) Match the verbs in A with the nouns in B.

A	B
1 take	a) a lot of fresh air
2 lose	
3 go on	b) exercises
4 get	c) weight
5 do	d) vitamins
	e) a diet

b) What are the four most important things to do if you want to stay healthy?
Example:
To be healthy you should walk every day.

c) People often *give up* things.
Example:
They stop smoking.
Sometimes they *cut down on* something. Example:
They smoke ten cigarettes a day, not twenty.

Colin Sullivan

Mr Sullivan has to lose weight and get fit. In your opinion what should he *give up* and what should he *cut down on?*

2 Work with a partner.

a) STUDENT A: Read Article A about Paul Smith, the fashion designer.
STUDENT B: Read Article B about Chris Eubank, the boxer.

A

I HAVE TO BE CAREFUL what I eat because I put on weight easily. I put on weight when I'm travelling, you know, all those meals on the plane, and snacks at airports. And I have a sweet tooth – I eat a lot of chocolate. But I don't worry about it. When I put on weight I just cut down on bread and eat less of everything.

I try to eat regularly. I always have toast and coffee before I leave home in the morning and I enjoy eating fresh fish and vegetables. I also take vitamin tablets. I like drinking water from the tap and I love good wine and champagne on special occasions.

On Sundays I swim for half an hour. I also enjoy cycling and running.

(from the *Sunday Express Magazine*)

B

AT THE MOMENT I'm healthier than any man in the street. I'm fit again, although I had chickenpox not long ago. I had a temperature of 102° and my face was swollen. Apart from colds and flu, chickenpox is the only illness I've had.

When we were children my mother gave us basic food like fish, rice, fresh vegetables and fruit. Junk food like hamburgers and sweets are expensive and we couldn't afford them. The kitchen is the most important room in the house because food is medicine. We weren't ill when we were children because we ate the right things.

Now I don't eat until after three in the afternoon because I like to train on an empty stomach.

I began smoking when I was six, but when I was sixteen my chest began to burn whenever I ran fast, so I gave up. My favourite drink is water or pineapple juice.

I don't feel as if I'm getting old yet – no grey hair and my teeth are all mine.

(from the *Evening Standard*)

b) Are these sentences *True* (T) or *False* (F) for your article?

1 He doesn't have breakfast.
2 He takes exercise.
3 He drinks alcohol.
4 He says he likes sweet food.
5 He has just been ill.
6 He gave up smoking.
7 He swims every Sunday.
8 He takes vitamins.

c) Compare your answers with your partner's answers. Ask questions about the other person and ask for more information. Example:
Why does/n't ..... have breakfast?

3 Look at the article about Chris Eubank. Find five words for parts of the body. What other words do you know?

4 Do people worry about health in your country? Is it different for men and women? If so how?

Vocabulary

Verbs often go with a particular noun. Which of these nouns go with *take?* Which go with *lose?* Examples:
lose weight, take exercise

1 an examination	6 a test
2 a football match	7 notes
	8 a bus
3 your temper	9 care
4 a chance	10 your way
5 an aspirin	

Writing

Improve your writing

Try not to use the same adjectives all the time. Don't always use *nice* or *good.*

a) Replace the words in italics below with one of the words in the box. Example:
We're having a *good* time here (we are doing nothing).
We're having a relaxing time here.

interesting	friendly
relaxing	attractive
comfortable	delicious

We arrived at the health club two days ago. There isn't a lot of food. It's *really nice* (it tastes good). The people are *nice* (everyone talks to each other). The bedrooms are *very nice* (there is everything you need). There is a very *nice* aerobics teacher here (he's good looking). I'm doing aerobics three times a day! The evening activities are *good* (there are a lot of things to do and learn about).

b) Make 4 sentences out of the 8 in Exercise a). Use each of these linking words once:
and, but, so, because.

GRAMMAR

Obligation and possibility

Have to and *can*

1 Karen has found an advertisement for a skiing holiday. She is phoning her brother, Sam, to tell him about it.

When do we have to pay?

Can we fly from Heathrow on Sunday?

a) Look at Sam's questions. Which verb form means *is it necessary?* and which means *is it possible?*

SKIING HOLIDAY IN ROMANIA
● HOLIDAY OF A LIFETIME! ●

2 weeks from only £400 (children under 2 free)

ALL YOU HAVE TO DO IS...

Pay £50 when you book. (You don't have to pay the other £350 until 2 weeks before you leave!)

WHAT DO YOU GET?

- Fly from Gatwick or Manchester airport on Sunday or Tuesday.
- Bed and breakfast in double rooms.
- Lunch and dinner at the hotel for a small extra charge.
- Ski slopes only 4 kilometres from hotel.
- Buses to ski slopes every 20 mins.
- Hire your ski equipment here. Make life easy!
- Ski classes every morning.

b) How do you think Karen answered Sam's questions? Read the advertisement and complete these sentences.

1 We _____ pay £50 when we book and then we _____ pay the other £350 until two weeks before we go.
2 We _____ fly on a Sunday, but we _____ fly from Heathrow. We _____ fly from Gatwick or Manchester.

2 Look at Exercise 1b) again.

a) How do we form:

1 positive and negative sentences and questions with *have to?*
2 positive and negative sentences and questions with *can?*

b) Check your answers in the *Language reference* on page 29.
c) Does the form of *have to* and *can* change when you use *he/she/it?*

3 Complete these sentences with the correct form of the verbs in brackets. Make negatives or questions if necessary.

1 My sister (can) _____ come to the party tonight because she (have to)_____ do her homework.
2 (we / have to) _____ pay for extra luggage on this flight?
3 They (can) _____ smoke in the classrooms, I'm afraid. They (have to) _____ go outside.

4 Imagine you are Karen and Sam. Practise the questions and answers. Replace the words in italics with (don't) have to or can('t). Example:

SAM: *Is it necessary for us* to take our own equipment?
 Do we have to take our own equipment?
KAREN: No, *it's possible for us* to hire it there.
 No, we can hire it there.

1 SAM: How much *is it necessary for us* to pay for the children?
 KAREN: *It's not necessary for you* to pay for Louise because she's under two.
2 SAM: When are the ski classes?
 KAREN: *It's possible for us* to have classes every morning.
3 SAM: *Is it possible for us* to walk to the ski slopes?
 KAREN: Well, *it's possible for you* to walk, but it's four kilometres.
4 SAM: *Is it necessary for us* to have all meals at the hotel?
 KAREN: No, but *it's possible* if you want to.

Using your grammar

1 Karen and Sam go to see the travel agent. They ask her some more questions about skiing in Romania.

a) [◻ 4.4] Listen and answer these questions.

 1 Can they hire a car there? 3 Do they have to get a visa?
 2 What can they do in the evenings?

b) Practise the questions and answers.

 1 How do we pronounce *can* and *have to* when they are weak?
 2 When is *can* not weak?

c) Work with a partner. Karen and Sam asked some more questions about the skiing holiday in Romania. What questions do you think they asked?

2 Talk about the rules for these things in your country. Examples:
In Britain you have to be eighteen to get married.
You can't drink alcohol in a pub before you're eighteen.

- getting married/divorced
- going to bars/nightclubs
- going to/leaving school
- joining the army
- carrying an identity card
- catching a plane
- voting
- driving a car

Obligation and advice
Should(n't) and must(n't)

1 Before Karen and Sam went skiing, people gave them lots of advice. Here are some examples. Which is stronger – *must* or *should*?

You must have health insurance.

You should take your own skis if possible. It's expensive to hire them.

You mustn't go later than March. There's no snow.

2 Give Sam and Karen more advice.

a) Use these notes and the words in brackets. Add any other words that are necessary. Example:
protect yourself from the sun / very hot (must)
You must protect yourself from the sun, because it's very hot.

 1 not eat at the hotel / food awful (should)
 2 buy traveller's cheques / difficult to change money (should)
 3 not take young children skiing / too dangerous (must)
 4 remember your camera / mountains fantastic (must)
 5 not pack formal clothes / very casual there (should)

b) [◻ 4.5] Listen and check your answers.

c) Listen again. Notice the weak pronunciation of *must* and *should* with /ə/. We don't pronounce the /t/ in *must* before a consonant. Example: *You **must** protect... /* jəməst prə'tekt /

27

VOCABULARY

At the doctor's

Look at the pictures. These people are waiting to see a doctor.

a) Match the sentences with the pictures.

He/She's:
1 got stomachache   4 got a rash
2 got a bad cold (or flu)   5 sprained his/her ankle
3 broken his/her arm

b) You've got all or some of the following symptoms. What's the matter with you?

> a cough   a runny nose   you're sneezing a lot
> a high temperature   a sore throat   a headache

c) What other words can replace the words in italics?

1 My *stomach* aches/hurts.   3 I've twisted/sprained/
2 I feel *awful*.   broken my *ankle*.

d) What should you do when you have any of the problems above? Use some of the words and expressions in the box. Example:
When you have a cold you should/must take an aspirin.

> an aspirin   vitamins   hot lemon juice   medicine
> lozenges   smoking   bed   lie down   an x-ray
> doctor   hospital

Using your vocabulary

1   Work with a partner. Take turns to be the doctor and the patient.

> PATIENT
> You don't feel well. Tell the doctor about your symptoms.
> Choose from these symptoms: *I can't sleep. I feel dizzy.*
> *I'm always sick when I eat. I have no energy. I've got spots.*

> DOCTOR
> Ask the patient for more information and give advice. Use *must*
> and *should*. Example:
> *Are you working too hard? Do you smoke? You must stop*
> *smoking. You should get more rest.*

2   What accidents or illnesses have you had?

a) What happened? How did you feel?
b) Work in groups. Talk about your accidents or illnesses.

USE AND REVIEW

1 Work with a partner.

STUDENT A: Look at page 126.

a) STUDENT B: Look at this puzzle.

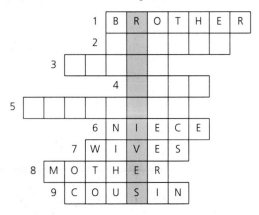

1	B	R	O	T	H	E	R	
2								
3								
4								
5								
6	N	I	E	C	E			
7	W	I	V	E	S			
8 M	O	T	H	E	R			
9 C	O	U	S	I	N			

Your partner will tell you about 2 – 5.
He/She won't tell you the words. He/She
will tell you *about* the words. Example:
1 *Not your sister* = BROTHER
b) Now tell Student A about 6 – 9.
c) Which word can you see in the pink box?

2 Work with a partner. You are going to write
a story about the pictures below.

a) Make notes for your story. Use the Past
Simple, the Past Continuous, linking words
(and, but, because, so) and time expressions
(when, while, in, at, on).
b) Tell your story to the class.
c) Now write the story. Check your work
carefully. Make sure the past forms of the
verbs are correct.

Language reference

1 *Have to*

FORM

Have to + base form of the verb

Positive		
I /You /We /They	**have to**	**work**.
He /She	**has to**	
Negative		
I /You /We /They **don't (do not)**	**have to**	**work**.
He /She **doesn't (does not)**	**have to**	
Question		
Do I /you /we /they	**have to**	**work**?
Does he /she		

USE

We use **have / has to** to talk about obligation, about
things that are necessary. It usually means that somebody
else (not the speaker) wants somebody to do something.
    In Britain you **have to** pay taxes. (It's the law).
We use **don't / doesn't have to** when we want to say
that something is not necessary.
    You **don't have to** do your homework now!

2 Modals

can must should could will shall would may

FORM

A modal verb comes before another verb (the main verb).
The main verb is always in the base form.

USE

Modal verbs have many different meanings. They always
tell us about the speaker's opinion. Here are some of the
different meanings of modal verbs from Units 1–4.

a) Possibility
    You **can** buy bread at that shop.
b) Asking for permission / requests
    Can I have your name?
    Could I borrow your pen?
    May I ask you a question?
c) Obligation / advice
    You **shouldn't** tell lies. (Obligation)
    You **should** wear warm clothes. (Advice)
    You **must** be careful. (Obligation/strong advice)
    You **mustn't** copy. (Obligation/strong advice)
d) Offers
    I'll (I **will**) carry that bag.
    Shall I help you?

•Getting around•

USE YOUR ENGLISH

Making travel arrangements

1   Look at the photographs on the right.

a) What do you do at these places? Example:
You catch a bus at a bus stop.

b) [📼 5.1]   Listen and match the conversations with the photographs.

c) Listen again. Make a list of words which are connected with transport. Example: *fare*.

d) Work with a partner. Compare your lists.

e) Add other words which are connected with transport.

2   Work with a partner.

a) Which forms of transport do you like/dislike? Use expressions like: *I love / hate / can't stand / don't mind going by bus.*

b) How would you like to travel in the future? Use expressions like: *I'd like / love to go in a helicopter / on a big ship.*

3   These two conversations are mixed up.

a) Put them in the correct order. The first line of each is done for you. Where did the conversations happen?

1
- Yes, change at Crewe. That's £43, please.　☐
- Single or return?　☐
- Could I have a ticket to Liverpool, please?　☐ 1
- Day return, please. Do I have to change?　☐
- Here you are. What platform does it leave from?
- Number 8.　☐

2
- Window, please. No smoking.　☐
- Yes, here you are.　☐
- Just these two cases. Is the flight on time?　☐
- Thank you. Would you like an aisle or window seat?　☐
- Yes, it is. Here's your boarding card. The flight is boarding at 10.20 from Gate 8.　☐
- Could I have your ticket and passport please?　☐ 1
- OK. And how much luggage have you got?　☐

b) [📼 5.2]   Listen and check your answers.

4   Work with a partner. STUDENT A, look at page 127. STUDENT B, look at page 128.

SKILLS

Listening and speaking

1 These pictures tell a true story about an old couple who were going to the seaside one day.

a) Work with a partner. What do you think happened?

b) Look at the map before you listen to the story. Find these places: Bristol, Clevedon, the M5 motorway, Tewkesbury.

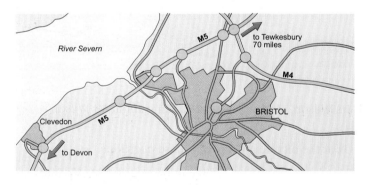

c) [📼 5.3] Listen. Was your story correct?

d) Listen again. Write true sentences about the story. Use these words to help you. Example: seaside / their old car
Thomas Brown and his wife were going to the seaside in their old car.

1 day trip / Devon
2 M5 / Clevedon / broke down
3 bus to Bristol / train to Tewkesbury
4 five hours later / the police / Mrs Brown / car

e) Tell the story again. Use the pictures to help you.

2 Someone is telling the same story to a friend.

a) [📼 5.4] Listen to extracts from the story. How many words are there in each sentence?

1 _____ seaside.
2 _____ legs.
3 _____ forgot _____.
4 _____ still waiting _____ car.

b) Listen again and complete the sentences.

c) Which words give the important information?

Vocabulary

We can use some words as nouns and verbs, or nouns and adjectives. The meanings are different. For example, *trip (n)* means a short journey but *trip (v)* means to catch your foot on something and fall.

a) Use a dictionary to find two different meanings of *train, fine* and *change.*

b) Complete these sentences. Use the correct form of one of the words above.

1 In Britain the weather _____ all the time. Sometimes it's sunny, sometimes it's cold.
2 Have you got _____ for £10?
3 My cousin is _____ to be a footballer.
4 When is the next _____ to London?
5 A: How are you feeling?
   B: _____, thanks.
6 The police _____ me because I was driving too fast.

Writing: reference words

1   Read the newspaper article below. What do the words in italics refer to?

1 *he* (line 3)   5 *she* (line 8)
2 *his* (line 3)   6 *him* (line 9)
3 *their* (line 5) 7 *them* (line 10)
4 *there* (line 7) 8 *they* (line 11)

Strange but true!

An Italian man stopped at a motorway service station to get some petrol. While *he* was paying for the petrol, *his* wife went to the toilet.
5 The man got back in *their* car and drove back home to Rome, 400 miles away. When he got *there* he spoke to his wife and realised *she* was missing. When reporters interviewed *him* he
10 told *them* that she usually slept in the back seat of the car and *they* never spoke anyway.

2   We use words like the ones in Exercise 1 so that we don't repeat the same word or expression. Change the words in italics in these sentences.

1 I know Bill and Tom. I met *Bill and Tom* last year.
2 It's a nice hotel. I've been *to the hotel.*
3 We saw Pete and Tim last night. We went to *Pete and Tim's* house.
4 A: Have you seen Dad?
   B: Yes, I saw *Dad* a few minutes ago.
5 A: Where are the boys?
   B: *The boys* are outside.

GRAMMAR

The future: plans, decisions and arrangements

1   Mrs Wilson, Max and Tess are talking about Mr Wilson's birthday.

a) Look at the picture and answer these questions.

1 Who has already decided about presents for Mr Wilson?
2 Who has just decided at the moment of speaking?

b) [🖭 5.5]   Listen. Were your guesses correct? What are they going to buy?

c) Which form of the future do we use:

1 when we talk about things we decide at the moment of speaking?
2 when we have made a plan or decision before we speak?
3 when we have made an arrangement?

d) Which is the best answer?

1 A: Do you want tea or coffee?
   B: I think *I'm going to / I'll* have tea, please.
2 A: Would you like to come to dinner on Friday?
   B: I'd love to, but *we're going / we'll go* on holiday tomorrow.
3 A: Have you got any change for the phone, please?
   B: Wait a minute, *I'll / I'm going* to have a look.
4 A: Do you want to go out tonight?
   B: No, I've decided *I'm going to / I'll* finish those letters tonight. They're already late.

2 Look at the *Language reference* on page 35. Check that you know how to form sentences with *will* and *going to*.

a) Complete the breakfast-time conversation at the Wilsons' house. Replace the verbs in brackets with *going to, will* or the Present Continuous.

MUM: I can't decide what to do this morning. Oh, I know, I *(do)* (1)_____ some work in the garden.

TESS: But, Mum, it's raining!

MUM: Is it? Oh! Well, that's not a problem. I *(put on)* (2)_____ my coat. And then I have to go out at two o'clock because I've got an appointment at the vet's. I *(take)* (3)_____ the cat for his flu injection.

TESS: I *(play)* (4)_____ badminton with Roger at 11 and then I *(buy)* (5)_____ a present for Dad. Max, are you OK?

MAX: No, I feel sick suddenly. I think I *(go)* (6)_____ back to bed. Tom *(have)* (7)_____ a party tonight and I want to feel OK for it. Tess ...?

TESS: All right. I *(buy)* (8)_____ the video for you. But I want the money first! If not, I *(not get)* (9)_____ it.

b) [5.6] Listen and check your answers.

3 Look at these extracts from Exercise 2.

a) Practise reading the sentences.

1 I'll **do** some work in the garden.
2 I'm **going to buy** a present for Dad.
3 If not, I **won't get** it.
4 I'm **playing** badminton with Roger at eleven.

b) [5.7] Listen and check your pronunciation.

c) Work with a partner. Practise reading the conversation in Exercise 2a). Be careful with your pronunciation.

Using your grammar

1 On New Year's Eve (31 December) many people make plans, or 'resolutions' for the New Year.

a) Imagine it is New Year's Eve. Write a list of five resolutions for yourself. What would you like to do? What are you going to do? Think about your job, health, appearance, money, relationships. Example:
I'm going to give up smoking and cycle to work every day.

b) Work in groups. Compare your resolutions.

2 [5.8] Listen to a poem.

a) Write what you hear.

b) Work with a partner. Compare your poems. Correct each other's work.

c) Write another poem with your partner. Complete the lines below.

> ## Tomorrow
> I'd really like to _____
> I think I _____
> I'm going to _____
> I'm _____ing _____ of course
> or am I? On second thoughts
> maybe I'll wait until the day
> after tomorrow.

d) Read your poem to the class.

VOCABULARY

Transport

1 Look at the pictures on the right.

a) Work with a partner. Which of these forms of transport is:

1 reliable?   3 fast?   5 comfortable?   7 healthy?
2 quiet?   4 cheap?   6 safe?   8 interesting?

b) What is the opposite of the adjectives in the box? Match them with four of the words in Exercise 1a) which have the opposite meaning. We form the opposites of the other four adjectives above with *un-*. Use a dictionary to help you.

dangerous   noisy   expensive   slow

2 Nouns and verbs which go together.

a) In each line there is one noun which does not go with the verb. Which one?

Verbs	Nouns
1 drive	a car, a plane, a train, a bus
2 ride	a bike, a boat, a horse, a camel
3 get on/off	a car, a plane, a horse, a train
4 get into/out of	a motorbike, a taxi, a car, a lorry
5 go by	bus, foot, car, helicopter

b) Match the verbs in A with the nouns in B. Sometimes there is more than one possibility.

A	B
1 to confirm ——————→	a) your flight
2 to reserve	b) your seat belt
3 to catch/miss	c) your luggage
4 to check in	d) a seat
5 to fasten	e) a plane

Using your vocabulary

1 Complete these sentences with information about yourself and your opinions.

1 I usually go to work / school by/ on _____.
2 My most exciting journey was _____.
3 The most awful trip I had was _____.

4 I think the most romantic way to travel is _____.
5 I think in the next century people will travel by/ on/ in _____.

2 Answer these questions.

1 Which forms of transport are popular in your country?
2 Think of two things which are good and two things which are bad about public transport in your country. Example:
   In Britain trains are fast but they are expensive.

USE AND REVIEW

1   Look at a–f below. Give the information in a different way. Use *have to, don't have to, can, can't, must, mustn't.* Example:
You mustn't lean out of the window.

(a) **DON'T LEAN OUT OF THE WINDOW**

(b) Best before 10.05.96

(c) **strawberry jam**
Keep in refrigerator after opening

(d) **P PAY AND DISPLAY**

(e) *Formal dress optional*

(f) **Hand wash only**

2   Work in groups and find the answers to these questions as quickly as possible.

1 you wear your watch on it   *your wrist*
2 your shoes go on them
3 you have ten of them
4 you hear with them
5 you can wear a belt round it
6 they get tired if you run
7 you smell with it
8 the dentist looks after them
9 people use this when they wait for a lift at the side of the road
10 you see with them

Language reference

The future

a) *Going to*

FORM

Be + going to + base form of the verb

Positive			
I'm (am) **You /We /They're (are)** **He /She /It's (is)**		**going to**	**play**.
Negative			
I'm not (am not) **You /We /They're not (are not)** **He /She /It's not (is not)**		**going to**	**play**.
Question			
Am **Are**	*I* *you /we /they*	**going to**	**play**?

USE

We use *going to* for plans and decisions which we have made before the moment of speaking.
    He's going to finish the painting tomorrow.

b) Present Continuous

FORM

(See Unit 2, page 15.)

USE

We use the Present Continuous for fixed personal arrangements in the future.

c) Present Continuous or *going to*?

We can use the Present Continuous or *going to* for future plans. The Present Continuous is better for definite plans and personal arrangements.
    We're leaving at 6 tomorrow.

d) *Will*

FORM

Will + base form of the verb

Positive
*I /You /We /They /He /She /It***'ll (will) come**.
Negative
I /You /We /They /He /She /It **won't** (**will not**) **come**.
Question
Will *I /you /we /they /he /she /it* **come**?

USE

We use *will* for decisions or plans which we make at the moment of speaking.
    I don't know what to do. I think I'll get a bus.

•Daily bread •

USE YOUR ENGLISH

Eating out

1 Anna and Liz are having a meal.

a) Match the verbs in A with the nouns in B.

A	B
1 take	a) the menu
2 pay	b) a tip
3 leave	c) your order
4 look at	d) the table
5 set	e) the bill

b) In what order do people usually do these things in a restaurant? Example:
First, you look at the menu.
Then the waiter/waitress ...

c) What is happening in each picture?

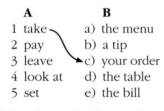

Starters
Prawn cocktail
Stuffed mushrooms
Soup of the day
Goat's cheese salad

Main courses
Fried cod or plaice
Grilled lamb chops
Spicy chicken
Ham, eggs and chips
Chicken in cream sauce
Chef's salad

2 Read parts of Anna and Liz's conversation with the waitress.

WAITRESS: _____ ?
LIZ: I think so. I'm going to have the chicken in cream sauce.
WAITRESS: _____ ?
LIZ: Er – salad, please. And some chips. I'm starving.
WAITRESS: And for you?
ANNA: _____. The mushrooms, I think.
WAITRESS: Fine. I'll just set the table for you.

(Later)
LIZ: _____ ?
WAITRESS: Certainly. Here you are.
LIZ: OK. That's £16.50.
ANNA: _____ ?
LIZ: No, it isn't. So that comes to about £18 including the tip. That's £9 each.
ANNA: _____ ?
LIZ: No, but you can pay by cheque.

a) Complete the conversation with these sentences.

1 I'll just have a starter.
2 Would you like salad or vegetables with that?
3 Are you ready to order yet?
4 Do they take Visa?
5 Could we have the bill, please?
6 Is service included?

b) [🖭 6.1] Listen and check your answers.
c) Work in groups of three. Practise reading the conversation.

3 Work with a partner. Look at the menu above. Take turns to be the waiter/waitress and the customer.

SKILLS

Reading and speaking

HOW TO EAT SPAGHETTI
BY ANTONIO CARLUCCIO

M y first memory of eating pasta is how much I loved sucking strings of spaghetti into my mouth. My mother told me
5 this wasn't polite. And when I used a spoon to get the spaghetti around the fork, she told me not to. But, apart from these basic rules, eating spaghetti is quite easy.

First, only use a spoon if the pasta is in a
10 soup or if it is very small in a sauce. For long thin pasta you have to be more careful.

If you're eating spaghetti, mix it with the sauce. If all the spaghetti is coated in sauce, it is easier to lift a few strings at a time. Then
15 push the pasta to the side of your plate to make space. Turn the fork so you have a mouthful on it which is not too big. When the forkful is tidy, put it into your mouth. Don't let the spaghetti hang out of your mouth.
20 You must never cut pasta with a knife. If you want, you can break spaghetti in half *before* you cook it.

There should not be too much sauce. When you've eaten the spaghetti, the plate
25 should be almost dry. Finally, don't put cheese over a fish pasta sauce.

(from *The Daily Mail*)

1 Look at the pictures of a man eating spaghetti.

a) Match the words in the box with the pictures.

> spoon and fork   cut/knife   turn/round a fork   suck

b) What is the man doing in each picture?
c) Which of these is not a polite way of eating spaghetti?
d) Read the article and check your guesses.
e) Which of the things in the pictures does or did Antonio do?
f) Answer these questions.

1 When is it all right to use a spoon to eat pasta?
2 What should you do to make spaghetti easier to lift?
3 What can you do (before cooking) to make spaghetti easier to eat?
4 How should the plate look when you have finished your spaghetti?
5 Antonio Carluccio says you must never use cheese with which sauce?

2 What are 'good table manners'? What are the rules in your country?

Vocabulary: setting the table

People in Britain usually set the table like this.

1 Name the things in the picture. Use a dictionary to help you.

2 If you look up the word *fork* in a good dictionary, you will find the pronunciation /fɔːk/. Look at the phonemic table on page 132 and practise the pronunciation of these words. How do you spell them?

1 /naɪf/   2 /spuːn/   3 /glɑːs/   4 /'næpkɪn/

3 How do you set the table in your country? Is it different from the British way?

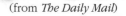

Writing: instructions

1   Antonio Carluccio's article on page 37 gives instructions for eating spaghetti.

a) Find some examples of instructions. Example:
Only use a spoon if the pasta is in a soup.

b) Use the words in the box to organise these instructions for eating prawns. Example:
5 = *First*

> First   Next   Then (x 2)
> After that   Finally

1 Dip it in mayonnaise or other dressing.
2 Pull the head off.
3 Wash your hands or clean them on a napkin.
4 Hold it by the head and pull the shell off.
5 Pick the prawn up.
6 Eat it with your fingers.

2   Think of something that is difficult to eat.

a) Write instructions for eating it. Do not say what it is.
b) Read your instructions to the class. The students must guess what you are describing.

GRAMMAR

Quantity expressions

A, some and any

> I've got **a** radio, **some** cassettes and **some** shampoo.

1   Name the things in Amy's suitcase and look at the box below.

> We use *a* and *some* in positive sentences. When do we use *a*? When do we use *some*? Check with the *Language reference* on page 41.

2   Do the things in the suitcase need *a* or *some?* Make two lists:
1 *A* cheque; 2 *Some* cassettes.

3   Complete the sentences with *a, some* or *any*. Look at the box below.

> *Amy hasn't got **any** soap.*
> *Has she got **any** clothes in her suitcase?*
>
> For plural countable nouns and for uncountable nouns we use *any* for negatives and (usually) for questions. Look at the *Language reference* on page 41 for questions with *some*.

1 I'm afraid I haven't got _____ sugar, but you can have _____ honey if you like.
2 Do you know if there are _____ good restaurants in Lincoln?
3 Would you like _____ coffee?
4 If you prefer, you could have _____ cup of tea.
5 They didn't have _____ information about the meeting on Wednesday.

A few, a little

May I borrow **a little** spaghetti?

Yes, you can have **a few** packets if you want!

4 Complete these sentences.

We use _____ for countable nouns and we use _____ for uncountable nouns in positive and negative sentences and questions.

A lot (of), much, many

He's got **a lot of** videos but **not many** books.

She's got **a lot of** work but **not much** time.

5 Complete these sentences.

We use _____ for countable and uncountable nouns in positive sentences.
We use _____ for countable nouns and _____ for uncountable nouns in negative sentences.

For more information see the *Language reference* on page 41.

6 Which is the correct expression?

1 I haven't got *much/many* money today.
2 I've got *a few/a little* fruit and *a lot of/many* vegetables.
3 They don't seem to have *much/many* free time these days.
4 He's only read *a few/a little* chapters of that new book, but he likes it.
5 A: Does he show *much/many* interest in sport?
  B: Yes, *a lot/a lot of*.

7 Amy is going away for a working weekend with Alice. Alice phones while Amy is packing her suitcase.

a) Look at Amy's suitcase again. Complete the conversation with words from the box. Sometimes there is more than one possibility.

| a some any much many a lot (of) |
| a little   a few |

ALICE: Have you packed _____ shampoo? I've run out.
AMY: Yes, but not _____. Why? Do you want _____ ?
ALICE: Yes, please. What about writing paper?
AMY: Well, I've got _____. How _____ do we need?
ALICE: _____. We have to write to all our clients. Oh, and we need stamps. I've only got _____ left.
AMY : It's OK. I've got _____ stamps.
ALICE: Don't forget to bring _____ cassettes for the car journey, will you?
AMY: Well, I haven't got _____. I usually listen to the radio.
ALICE: And I forgot to go to the bank. I hope you remembered to get _____ money?
AMY: No, I didn't. You've got _____ cheque book, haven't you?

b) [🔲 6.2]   Listen and check your answers.

Using your grammar

1 Imagine a person from another country is coming to visit your home.

a) You want to give him/her a meal that is typical of your country. You can have a big meal with different dishes or just one dish. Choose your menu.
b) Write a list of what you need for the meal. The exact quantities don't matter.

2 Work with a partner.

STUDENT A: Look at page 127.
STUDENT B: Look at page 128.

VOCABULARY

Food and drink

1 Look at the food in the picture.

a) Make four lists: 1 Fruit; 2 Vegetables; 3 Fish; 4 Meat. Use a dictionary to help you. Mark the stressed syllable on each word. Example: Fruit: 'strawberries.

b) Add other words to each list.

2 Look at the cooking equipment on the right.

a) Match the pictures with the words in the box.

> oven   grill   frying-pan   saucepan

b) Which equipment do we use to:

1 roast?   2 fry?   3 boil?   4 bake?   5 grill ?

Match the pictures with one of these verbs. Sometimes there is more than one possibility.

c) Work with a partner. Which do you like – roast, fried, boiled, baked or grilled food? Tell your partner. Example: *I love roast chicken and grilled peppers.*

Using your vocabulary

1 Read the article and answer these questions.

1 How many meals does Deborah have in a day?
2 What is the name of each meal?
3 What snacks does she eat?

2 Work with a partner.

a) Ask him/her about the food and drink he/she ate yesterday.

b) Make a list of all the meals and the snacks.

c) Write a paragraph about your partner.

DAILY BREAD
•••••••••••••••••••
DEBORAH BULL

WHAT THE ROYAL BALLET'S PRINCIPAL DANCER ATE YESTERDAY

'I always have breakfast. Yesterday it was plain low-fat yoghurt with unsweetened muesli without any nuts, a banana and tea with milk. I had a class from 10.30 to 11.45, and I always keep water and a banana to hand because bananas are very good for energy. Then there was a break, and I had an apple and a cup of tea. I had a rehearsal from 12 to 2.30 – and then I ate a banana. For lunch I had two biscuits with cheese and a plain yoghurt. Nothing else apart from some tea and more water until dinner time. Dinner was a green salad, just lettuce with an oil and vinegar dressing, pasta with home-made tomato sauce and Parmesan cheese. A glass of white wine and more water. No pudding – I rarely eat puddings. Nothing else.'

(from *The Independent on Sunday*)

USE AND REVIEW

the best of SOUTH AFRICA

Stay in a top quality hotel near a world famous wildlife park. Enjoy the beauty of Africa and the magnificent coast. Excellent opportunities for walking, photography and swimming.

ITALY

Visit the galleries and museums of Florence. Eat wonderful food and drink the delicious local wines in this beautiful city. Go shopping for the best clothes in the world.

SINGAPORE AND MALAYSIA

Visit exotic Singapore with its shops and lively nightlife. Then choose from the amazing sights Malaysia offers. You could trek through the tropical jungle, visit the charming towns on the coast, or relax on the famous beaches of Penang.

▄ BRITAIN ▄

Small friendly hotel on the south coast of Devon. Excellent beach, good walking, riding and golf nearby.

1   Look at these advertisements for holidays.

a)   You can go on holiday to one of these places. Which place would you like to go to? Plan your holiday. Think about these things.

1 What are you going to take with you?
2 How are you going to travel when you are there?
3 What do you want to do there?
4 What would you like to eat and drink?
5 What souvenirs will you bring back?

b)   Work in groups. Compare your plans.

2   Find ten more words connected with transport.

```
Z U H O R S E N R H
M N C B I C Y C L E
C D T G P H W L X L
A E R O P L A N E I
M R Q R U S K F D C
E G F N B V C E M O
L R E T A X I R S P
C O A C H I T R E T
H U S B J L F Y G E
O N L U E Y E C A R
B D R S B B O A T A
```

Language reference

Quantity expressions

a) Countable and uncountable nouns

Some nouns are countable (*door, pen, book*) and others are uncountable (*milk, paper, shampoo*).
a) We can use countable nouns in the singular with an indefinite article (*a* door) and also in the plural (*two* pens, *some* books).
b) We can't use uncountable nouns with the indefinite article or in the plural (*some* milk NOT ~~a milk~~).

b) *Some, any*

We use *some* and *any* to talk about quantity, but not a particular quantity.
a) We use *some* in positive sentences with uncountable nouns (*some* shampoo) and plural countable nouns (*some* books).
b) We also use *some* for requests, questions and offers when we expect the answer 'yes'.
   A: *Would you like* ***some*** *tea?*   B: *Yes, I'd love some.*
   A: *Can I have* ***some*** *paper?*   B: *Of course you can.*
c) We use *any* with plural countable nouns and uncountable nouns for questions when we do not know the answer and for negative sentences.
   Have you got ***any*** *brothers or sisters?*
   I didn't buy ***any*** *bread.*

c) *A few, a little*

We use *a few* and *a little* to talk about a small quantity.
a) We use *a few* with countable nouns in questions and positive sentences.
   You can have ***a few*** *sweets.*
b) We use *a little* with uncountable nouns in questions and positive sentences.
   May I have ***a little*** *more tea?*
   I can give you ***a little*** *chocolate.*

d) *A lot (of), much, many*

We use *a lot (of), much* and *many* to talk about a large quantity.
a) We use *a lot (of)* with countable and uncountable nouns in positive and negative sentences and questions.
   Are you doing ***a lot of*** *work at the moment?*
   He's got ***a lot of*** *free time.*
   I've got some cassettes, but not ***a lot***.
b) We use *much* with uncountable nouns in negative sentences and questions.
   I'm afraid I don't have ***much*** *time.*
c) We use *many* with countable nouns in negative sentences and questions.
   We didn't have ***many*** *sunny days.*

We don't usually use *much* in positive sentences. In informal English, *many* is not common in positive sentences. We prefer *a lot (of).*

•How do you feel about...? •

USE YOUR ENGLISH

Saying what you think

1 Judy and Andrew are going to choose posters for their rooms at university.

a) Make three lists of the words in the box: 1 Good; 2 Bad; 3 Not good or bad.

| great | not bad | fantastic | awful | lovely |
| all right | nice | wonderful | dreadful | boring |

b) Look at the posters. What do you think of them? Give your reasons. Use some of the words in the box above. Example:
I think the second poster's lovely!

2 [▭ 7.1] Listen to Judy and Andrew's conversation about the posters. They are each going to buy one poster. Which one do you think Judy will buy? Which will Andrew buy?

3 [▭ 7.2] Listen to parts of Judy and Andrew's conversation.

a) Complete the sentences.

  1 JUDY: I _____ the first poster _____, I'm afraid.
               It's _____, but ...
    ANDREW: Really? I think _____!
  2 ANDREW: I _____ the picture of the man and the baby.
    JUDY: I _____ it. It's _____ !
  3 JUDY: This one is _____. It _____ calm and relaxed.
    ANDREW: Yes, it's _____ . But it's not really _____ .

b) Work with a partner and practise the conversations.

4 [▭ 7.3] Listen to five pieces of music. How do you feel about them? Example:
The first piece is wonderful! I love jazz.

5 Work in groups. Think of different types of music, films, food, books and TV programmes.

a) Which do you like? Which don't you like? Make two lists.
b) Go round the class and find people who agree and disagree with you.
c) Report back to the class.

a

b

DOMINIQUE ISSERMANN

c

SKILLS

Speaking and listening

1 Which of these ages is the best? Which is the most difficult? Why?

0-5   6-12   13-18

TEENAGE MOTHERS: WHAT CAN WE DO?

More than a million school leavers without jobs

NUMBER OF HOMELESS TEENAGERS GOES UP

2 Look at the headlines above from British newspapers. What problems do young people in Britain have these days?

3 What do parents and young people usually argue about? Is it different for boys and girls?

4 Which of these are most important for teenagers? Make two lists of five: 1 For boys; 2 For girls. Add some of your ideas.

- relationship with parents
- clothes and appearance
- politics
- going out
- relationships and marriage
- smoking
- housework
- money
- the environment

5 [📼 7.4.] Chris and Penny are seventeen. They are talking about their problems.

a) Listen and look at the list in Exercise 4. Which things do they talk about?

b) What do Chris and Penny say? Use the words in the box to write sentences. Example:
Penny says it's dangerous to go out in the sun these days.

sun	meat	fashion	red	11 o'clock	college
twenty-eight	two	boring			

c) Listen again and check your answers.

6 Did Chris and Penny say anything to surprise you?

Vocabulary: guessing words in context

Chris and Penny used some of the expressions below. Read the tapescript on page 139 carefully. Can you guess the meaning of these expressions? Is it a) or b)?

1 My Dad *is fed up.* (line 9)
  a) has eaten too much
  b) is unhappy

2 He hopes I'll *change my mind.* (line 11)
  a) become more intelligent
  b) think differently

3 They like me to look *smart.* (line 18)
  a) tidy and clean
  b) intelligent

4 I go to *second-hand* shops. (line 21)
  a) shops which are not very good
  b) shops which sell things which aren't new

5 *dye* my hair (line 24)
  a) cut it off
  b) change the colour

6 *picks me up* (line 31)
  a) comes and gets me
  b) lifts me up

Writing: *the*

Penny said these things:

Young people have to learn to be independent.
The boys at my school all smoke.

In the first sentence she was talking about young people **in general**, so she didn't use *the*.
But in the second sentence she was talking about **particular** boys, the boys at her school.

1   Read these sentences. Cross out *the* if it isn't necessary.

1 I spend all my money on the books.
2 The books on this shelf are quite useful.
3 The water is very good for your health.
4 The water in this country tastes awful.
5 She doesn't usually like the Indian food.
6 The Indian food in that restaurant is great.

2   A student wrote this paragraph. There are four mistakes with *the*. Can you find them?

All over the world the women still do not have the same opportunities as the men. The men in my office always get better jobs. The young people in my country worry about the jobs and the money.

3   Write a letter to a newspaper about the problems of young people in your country. Be careful with *the*.

GRAMMAR

Present Perfect Simple

Dear Mum,
Well, the good news is that we're here! We moved in on Monday. The bad news is that the furniture hasn't arrived yet so we have to sleep on the floor. We're still painting the sitting room but we've borrowed a CD player so we can listen to music while we're working. A friend has just given us some curtains for the sitting room but we haven't put them up yet. I've never put up curtains before so I hope they don't fall down! We've also got a carpet. We bought it in a sale yesterday, but we haven't laid it yet. Perhaps you can help us when you come. Have you ever laid a carpet?

David and Louise have just moved into their new flat.

a) Read part of Louise's letter to her mother.
b) Look at the letter again. Do we know the answers to these questions?

1 When did David and Louise move into their new house?
2 When did they borrow a CD player?
3 When did they get the curtains?
4 When did they buy the carpet?

c) When Louise writes about **when** things happen, does she use the Past Simple or the Present Perfect? Find some examples.
d) When the **event** (not **when** it happened) is important to Louise, does she use the Past Simple or the Present Perfect? Find some examples.
e) Have David and Louise finished painting the sitting room yet?

Present Perfect and Past Simple

1   Two days later Louise's mother telephoned.

a) What questions do you think Louise's mother asked? Use these words to make questions.

1 furniture / arrive / yet? When / come?
2 finish / painting the sitting room / yet?
3 put up / curtains / yet?
4 lay / carpet / yet?

b) [🔲 7.5]   Listen and check your answers. Then write Louise's answers.

2   What are the Past Simple and the Past Participles of these verbs: see, drink, do, put, speak, begin, write, go, meet, eat? Use the Irregular Verb list on page 132 to help you.

3   Which is the correct verb in these sentences?

1 *I've seen / I saw* that play last week.
2 Oh, you've got the new Le Carré novel. *Have you finished / did you finish* it? If so, can I borrow it?
3 The taxi *arrived / has arrived*. I must go.
4 *I've been / I went* to Disneyland when I was a child.
5 *I've done / I did* my homework at last. I'm very pleased.
6 Oh no, *I've lost / I lost* my earring.

Time expressions with the Present Perfect

We often use the adverbs *just, ever, never* and *yet* with the Present Perfect.

a) Look at Louise's letter again. Complete these sentences.

1 We use _____ in questions to ask about past experience. Example:
Have you _____ laid a carpet?
2 We use _____ in the negative to talk about past experience. Example:
I've _____ put up curtains before.
3 We use _____ with questions and negatives to ask and talk about the time up to now. Example:
Has the furniture arrived _____ ?
The furniture hasn't arrived _____ .
4 We use _____ to talk about something which happened a short time ago. Example:
A friend's _____ given us some curtains.

b) Check your answers in the *Language reference* on page 47.

Using your grammar

1 [🔲 7.6]   Listen.

a) Write down the sentences.
b) In which two sentences is there **not** a Present Perfect?
c) What are *he's* and *it's* short for?

2   Louise is throwing some of her things away. Look at the picture. What has she done in her life? Example:
She has climbed Mount Everest.

3   Work with a partner.

a) Ask about his/her experiences. Use the ideas below and your own ideas. Example:
see / a ghost
A: *Have you ever seen a ghost?*
B: *Yes, I have.*
A: *Oh, tell me about it.*
B: *Well, two years ago ...*

1 ride / a donkey
2 have / a fight
3 spend / a lot of money
4 win / a prize

b) Report back to the class.

VOCABULARY

Feelings and opinions

1 We often use *-ed* adjectives to talk about feelings.
Look at the pictures. How do the people feel? Choose words from
the box. Example: Picture 1 = *He's bored.*

frightened   bored   embarrassed   excited
depressed   surprised

2 We use *-ing* adjectives to talk about our opinions. Look at
Picture 1 again. We can also say *he's boring.* This adjective
describes our opinion of him. Look at all the pictures again. Use
-ing adjectives to describe the people's opinions.

    1 The film is *boring.*   5 The news is _____ .
    2 The phone call is _____ . 6 The visit to the supermarket
    3 His birthday is _____ .   is _____ .
    4 The noise is _____ .

3 Change the verbs in brackets into adjectives. Use the *-ed* or
the *-ing* form.

1 I felt _____ when he wasn't on the last bus. *(worry)*
2 I'm glad to get home, because it was a very _____ day. *(tire)*
3 The book was very _____ so I read it from cover to cover.
   (interest)
4 I was really _____ with Joe when he forgot to phone me.
   (annoy)

Using your vocabulary

How do *you* feel about things? Think about your personal life and
things which are happening in the world.

1 Complete these sentences.

1 I feel depressed when …   4 … is/are boring.
2 … is/are really interesting. 5 I sometimes feel worried about …
3 I am frightened of …   6 It's embarrassing when …

2 Write more sentences using other *-ing* or *-ed* adjectives.

3 Go round the class. What do people find
depressing/interesting/frightening? Make a list. Then report back
to the class.

USE AND REVIEW

1   Choose one of the Bingo boards. Make questions for each square. (Example: *Do you eat much meat?*) Go round the class and find people who can answer them. Write the names in the squares. When you have completed a line (across, down or diagonally) shout *Bingo!*

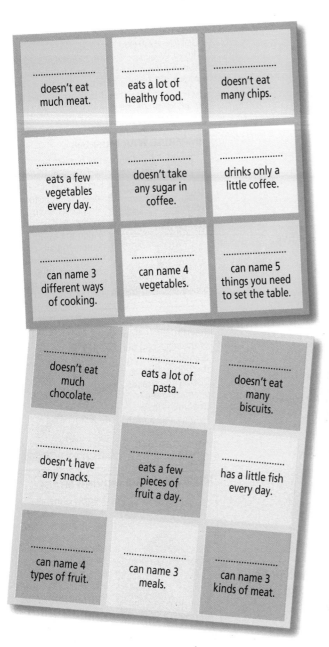

2   Now ask people more questions. If Nicolas said he didn't eat much meat, for example, ask him for more information. Example: *Why don't you eat much meat?*

Language reference

1 Present Perfect Simple

FORM

The auxiliary *has / have* and the past participle of the verb.

Positive
We'**ve** (**have**) **eaten** Indian food.
Negative
She **hasn't** (**has not**) eaten Indian food.
Question
Have they **finished**? Yes, they **have**. (NOT ~~Yes, they've.~~) **Has** she **finished**?   No, she **hasn't**.

USE

We use the Present Perfect Simple to talk about the past when it is connected with the present. For example:

a) Recent changes: past events with results in the present.
   John's eaten too much. He isn't hungry now.

b) Experience: past experiences which are important to the speaker at the time of speaking. It is not important *when* something happened.
   I've been to Spain.
   She's never met the Queen.
   I've eaten paella twice.

We use the Past Simple when we are thinking of when something happened.
   I went to Spain in 1990.

2 Indefinite time expressions

We often use the Present Perfect with adverbs like *yet, never, ever* and *just* to talk about the past, where the exact time is not important.

a) *Yet* means in the time up to now. We use it at the end of the sentence with negatives and questions.
   *Has he gone **yet**? He hasn't spoken **yet**.*

b) *Ever /never* means at any time in the past.

c) *Just* means a short time ago.

I've	never	been to India.
	just	
Have you	ever	been to India?
	just	

• All work and no play...•

USE YOUR ENGLISH

Making arrangements

1 Diane and Mark are talking on the phone.

a) Look at the film advertisement on the right. Use the information to complete their conversation.

DIANE: Do you fancy seeing *Four Weddings and a Funeral* tonight?
MARK: I don't know anything about it. Who's in it?
DIANE: _____.
MARK: What's it about?
DIANE: _____.
MARK: It sounds good. Where's it on?
DIANE: _____.
MARK: OK. I've got a meeting that finishes at half past five. What time does the film start?
DIANE: _____.
MARK: Let's go to the early show, shall we?
DIANE: All right. Shall we try that new Italian pizza place afterwards? My sister says it's great.
MARK: Fine. Why don't we meet at the cinema at ten past six?

b) [🖭 8.1] Listen and check your answers.

c) Look at the conversation again and answer these questions.

1 What is an informal way of saying *Would you like to see?*
2 *Let's* go to ..... is one way of making a suggestion. Find two more ways.

2 Look at the other advertisements.

a) Where would you go if you were interested in:

1 film and television?   3 fish?
2 aeroplanes?   4 exciting rides?

b) Work with a partner. Choose one of the places in the advertisements. Take turns to invite each other out. Accept or refuse the invitation. If you refuse make an excuse. Example:
A: *Do you fancy going to .....?* OR *Would you like to go to .....?*
B: *I'd love to.* OR *I'm afraid I can't tonight. I have to work.*

c) Suggest how to get there and where to meet. Example:
A: *Why don't we meet at the cinema?*
B: *Fine. I'll see you at six.*

FOUR WEDDINGS AND A FUNERAL (15)
ODEON, HARLOW
Progs: Weekdays 6.15. 8.20 Sunday 8.20
Starring Hugh Grant & Andie McDowell
A love story with a difference. Bachelor Hugh Grant, in his twenties, has never wanted to marry. Then he meets Andie McDowell! A sparkling comedy with great music.

IMPERIAL WAR MUSEUM

The biggest and best aeroplane museum in Europe. Visit our huge collection of historic aeroplanes, from Spitfires to Concorde. Watch the flying demonstrations or take a flight yourself! Open from 10–6. Flying demonstration daily at 3 pm.

SEALIFE CENTRE

Travel to the bottom of the sea along our dramatic walk-through tunnel. Discover thousands of amazing sea creatures – from shrimps and starfish to octopuses and sharks. Open daily from 10 am.

MUSEUM OF THE MOVING IMAGE

Lights...cameras... action. Discover the fascinating world of film and television. Museum of the Moving Image is entertainment and education. 'Fly' over the River Thames like Superman – have a Hollywood film test.

ALTON TOWERS

Enjoy all the fun of the rides and much, much more! There are shows, street entertainment, fireworks, shops and restaurants.

SKILLS

Reading and listening

1 In Britain people deliver letters, newspapers and milk to homes in the morning. Irene Hall won the award for the best milkperson of the year.

a) Look at the newspaper headline. What did she do to win the award? Can you guess?

b) Read the first part of an article about Irene. Was your guess correct?

She delivers kindness with the milk

'We always wake up at 3.50 am even on Sundays. My husband, Ken, is a milkman too. We don't need an alarm clock because I can wake whenever I want. I don't mind getting up in the middle of the night. You know that so many people are depending on you to have the milk on their doorsteps before breakfast. We've finished by 8.30 am and then we have the rest of the day to ourselves. We don't go to bed early but I usually get five hours' sleep a night.

Our customers have become our friends. They leave cakes and home-grown vegetables out for us. We talk to them on Friday afternoons when we call to collect the money. There are some elderly people we keep an eye on. We have keys to their homes and we check they're all right. Sometimes they leave us little notes asking us to do little jobs for them. We've done all sorts of things, from posting letters to peeling potatoes.'

(from *The Independent*)

c) Read the article again and answer these questions.

1 What time does Irene wake up?
2 How does she feel about getting up early?
3 What time does she finish work?
4 How long does she sleep?
5 What presents do customers give her?
6 When does she collect the money from the customers?
7 Who does Irene look after?
8 Why does she have keys to their homes?
9 What kind of jobs does she do for them?

2 [🔲 8.2] Irene is talking about her job. Listen and then read the rest of the article and find five mistakes.

Irene's three sons are also milkmen. When they were young she had to leave them at home while she was working.

Irene is a little nervous of being out at night. Everything is very quiet. When she goes down the street she never sees other people but she sometimes sees small animals like ducks or squirrels.

She has only had one day off work – when she went to London to get her award.

Vocabulary: opposites

Irene says, '*The streets are really quiet at night.*' The opposite of *quiet* is **noisy**.

a) Choose a word from the box which is the opposite of the word in italics.

generous	poor	safe
wrong	light	difficult
dirty	expensive	

1 A: I thought the exam was really *easy*.
   B: Did you? I thought it was quite _____.
2 A: Number 2 is *right*.
   B: No, it isn't. It's _____.
3 A: I think Fred's rather *mean*.
   B: Do you? Why? I think he's quite _____.
4 A: This room is really *clean* now.
   B: I think it's still _____.
5 A: This city is really *dangerous*.
   B: I think it's quite _____.
6 A: Can you carry this bag? It's *heavy*.
   B: No, it isn't. It's _____.
7 A: It's quite *cheap* to live in Britain.
   B: You're joking! It's very _____.
8 A: I believe you're incredibly *rich*.
   B: No, actually I'm very _____ now.

b) [🔲 8.3] Listen to the first three of the conversations above.
Which word does B always stress? Why?

Writing: formal and informal letters

1 Read the job advertisement below. Then read Andrew Walter's formal letter of application for the job. Choose the correct sentences, a) or b).

WWF World Wide Fund For Nature needs volunteers to work with mountain gorillas in Central Africa (for at least 1 year). Experience not necessary but you must be interested in the preservation of gorillas and their habitats. You should also be young, single, healthy and speak English and French.
Successful applicants will receive a grant to cover airfare and living expenses. Please apply in writing to Karl Rosen.

34 Highgate Park,
Lancaster
LB2 4RT
5th March 1995

Dear Mr Rosen,

1 a) I saw your ad about working with mountain gorillas.
   b) I am writing with reference to your advertisement in the Daily News.

2 a) I am twenty-eight years old and single.
   b) I'm 28. I'm not married.

3 a) I'm afraid I haven't had any experience with these animals but I would like to learn.
   b) Sorry, I haven't worked with gorillas, but I'd love to try.

4 a) My French isn't bad and I'm really fit.
   b) I can communicate quite well in French and my health is very good.

5 a) Send me an application form when you can.
   b) I would be grateful if you could send me an application form as soon as possible, please.

6 a) Yours sincerely,
   b) Best wishes,

Andrew Walter

Andrew Walter

2 Imagine you want to go and work with mountain gorillas.

a) Write a short letter in answer to the advertisement above. Give information about yourself.

b) Work with a partner. Read each other's letters and try to improve them.

GRAMMAR

Verbs followed by *-ing* or *to*

Andrew Walter, 28, who is planning to give up his well-paid job as a computer programmer to go and work with mountain gorillas in Africa.

1 [🔊 8.4] Listen to part of a radio interview with Andrew.

a) Complete these sentences.

1 He's decided _____ his house.
2 He wants _____ something different.
3 He'd like _____ how the gorillas live.
4 He hopes _____ a book.
5 He needs _____ something useful.
6 He doesn't mind _____ in difficult conditions.
7 He'll miss _____ his friends.
8 He has promised _____ to them every week.

b) Which verbs are followed by *to?* Which verbs are followed by *-ing?* Make two lists of verbs from Exercise 1a).

2   Read part of a newspaper article about Andrew and answer the questions below.

Andrew Walter has always been interested in watching films and TV programmes on animals. He also enjoys taking photographs of them. That's why he has given up his job and is going to Central Africa where he will help to look after the endangered gorilla population. "I was delighted to accept the offer. I am fed up with working in an office and very excited to have such a wonderful opportunity to change my life." He expects to fly out next month when he has finished making all the arrangements.

a)   Are the verbs *enjoy, help, expect, finish* followed by -*ing* or *to?* Add them to your list.

b)   Which prepositions follow the adjectives *interested* and *fed up?*

c)   Which form of the verb follows prepositions, -*ing* or *to?*

d)   Which form of the verb follows the adjectives *delighted* and *excited*, -*ing* or *to?*

3   Read these sentences.

a)   Complete them with one of these prepositions: *about, on, with, of* or *at.* Don't look at the verbs in brackets yet.

1 She's bored _____ television.   *(watch)*
2 She's frightened _____ the dark.   *(sleep in)*
3 I'm worried _____ the exam.   *(do)*
4 He's keen _____ gorillas.   *(work with)*
5 He's thinking _____ his job.   *(give up)*
6 She's really good _____ English.   *(speak)*

b)   Make sentences with the verbs in brackets. Example:
She's bored with watching television.

4   Complete this letter that Andrew sent home. Change the verbs in brackets to the -*ing* or *to* form. Use the *Language reference* on page 53 to help you.

It's so great (be) (1)_____ here! I have managed
(find) (2)_____ a flat already, and someone has offered
(help) (3)_____ me find a second-hand car. I really love
(work) (4)_____ with the gorillas. It's so interesting
(see) (5)_____ how they live together and every day I try
(remember) (6)_____ everything I see so that I can write
it down later. I want (stay) (7)_____ here forever.
I'll be quite sad (come) (8)_____ back. I'm sorry I
forgot (write) (9)_____ earlier. I promise
(phone) (10)_____ soon.

Using your grammar

1   Work in groups to tell a story. Begin: *One sunny morning Paul and Jill got into their car and set off on a trip.*

Each person in the group should add a sentence to the story, using one of the verbs in the box. Use each verb once.

decide	forget	stop
like	want	would like
miss	help	need	enjoy
don't mind	manage	try
promise	offer	hope
need		

Before you start, choose a secretary. He/She should write the story. If someone makes a mistake with the verb form they are out of the game. The winner is the last person to be out.

2   Work with a partner. Choose one of the pictures above. Describe it but don't say the name. Your partner must guess the name of the thing. Use the verbs in the box. Example: *It's expensive to buy.*

look after	drive	buy
use	have	drink	ride

VOCABULARY

What do you do?

1   Complete these sentences. Use a dictionary to help you.

Someone who:
1 flies planes is a *p*_____.
2 helps people with their money is
  an *a*_____.
3 organises holidays is a *t*_____ _____.
4 takes photographs is a *p*_____.
5 works in politics is a *p*_____.

6 writes for a newspaper is a *j*_____.
7 repairs cars is a *m*_____.
8 works in the theatre is an *a*_____.
9 works in a library is a *l*_____.
10 designs buildings is an *a*_____.
11 plans machines, roads bridges is an *e*_____.

2   Look at the words in Exercise 1.

a)   How many syllables does each word have?
Make three lists: 1 Words of two syllables
(pilot); 2 Words of three syllables *(architect);*
3 Words of four syllables *(travel agent).*

b)   Add other jobs you know to the list.

c)   [🔲 8.5]   The stress in the words in
Exercise 2a) comes on the first syllable. Listen
and mark the stressed syllable in the other
words from Exercise 1. Example: *a'ccountant.*

3   Which jobs do you think are :

boring   exciting   interesting
romantic   well-paid   stressful
dangerous   fun   important

4   Which jobs can you imagine doing? Why?

5   Which jobs would you hate to do? Why?

Using your vocabulary

1   There is a proverb in English *All work and no play makes*
Jack a dull boy. (Dull = not interesting)

a)   How long is a typical working day in your country?
b)   Which jobs get the highest and lowest salaries? Why?

2   Do this quiz with a partner.

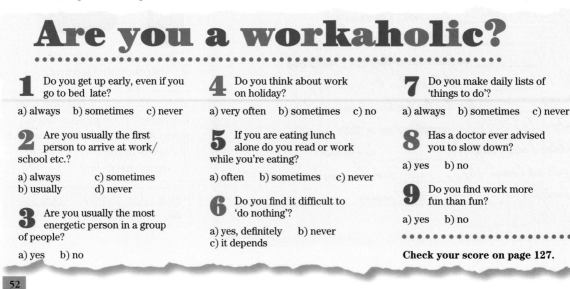

Are you a workaholic?

1 Do you get up early, even if you go to bed late?

a) always   b) sometimes   c) never

2 Are you usually the first person to arrive at work/ school etc.?

a) always   c) sometimes
b) usually   d) never

3 Are you usually the most energetic person in a group of people?

a) yes   b) no

4 Do you think about work on holiday?

a) very often   b) sometimes   c) no

5 If you are eating lunch alone do you read or work while you're eating?

a) often   b) sometimes   c) never

6 Do you find it difficult to 'do nothing'?

a) yes, definitely   b) never
c) it depends

7 Do you make daily lists of 'things to do'?

a) always   b) sometimes   c) never

8 Has a doctor ever advised you to slow down?

a) yes   b) no

9 Do you find work more fun than fun?

a) yes   b) no

Check your score on page 127.

USE AND REVIEW

Mediterranean weather hits Britain. Man in hospital with sunstroke

Woman finds strange object in park

STUDENT OF THE YEAR AWARD

POP STAR IN SECRET MARRIAGE CEREMONY

1 Look at the newspaper headlines above.

a) Work with a partner. Write a story about one of the headlines. Give more information. What happened? Why? When? Where? How? Example:

> A student at the York School of Languages has won the award for the student of the year.
> Polish student Danuta Gorecka has never been late, never missed a lesson and has always been a cheerful and co-operative member of the class. She has made so much progress that she has gone from elementary to upper intermediate level in just six months! Danuta came to Britain six months ago because

b) Work in groups. Look at the other students' stories and try to improve them.

2 Work with your partner again. Imagine you are going to present your story on television.

STUDENT A	STUDENT B
You are the television presenter. Read your story. Then interview the person (or one of the people) involved in the story.	You are the person in the story. Answer the interviewer's questions. How do/did you feel?

Example:
TV PRESENTER: *Danuta, how do you feel about winning this award?*
DANUTA: *Well, I'm very excited, but I also feel a little nervous, because ...*

3 Present your news stories in groups.

Language reference

-ing or *to?*

a) Verbs followed by *-ing*

Some of the most common verbs are:

enjoy	love*	not mind
finish	can't stand	give up
fancy	miss	suggest
like*		

*They enjoy **working** there.*
*Note that the *to* form of the verb can also follow these verbs with only a very small change in meaning.

b) Verbs followed by *to* + base form

Some of the most common verbs are:

decide	learn	refuse
expect	manage	try
forget	need	want
help	offer	would like
hope	promise	

*He decided **to go** to West Africa.*

c) Adjectives followed by *to* + base form

The *to* form of the verb usually follows adjectives.
> *I'm really **pleased to see** you.*
> *It's really **interesting to go** to different countries.*

d) Prepositions followed by *-ing*

The *-ing* form of the verb usually follows prepositions.
> *He's good **at cooking**.*
> *They're interested **in learning** to fly.*

•A place of your own•

USE YOUR ENGLISH

Talking about preferences

1 Look at the pictures of different homes.

a) Match the advertisements with the pictures.
b) Where would you like to live? Give your
reasons. Example:
I'd prefer to live in a flat near the sea because ...

Ⓐ *Spacious semi-detached house just outside the town. Large back garden, three bedrooms.*

Ⓑ Small modern flat in city centre. Kitchen/dining room, small sitting-room, 1 bedroom, bathroom.

Ⓒ 2 bedroomed modern bungalow near the sea. Garden, garage.

Ⓓ 19th century farmhouse in beautiful Derbyshire country-side. 4 bedrooms, large sitting room, extensive gardens.

2 Look at these people. Which of the homes on the right do
you think they would choose?

a b c

a) [🖭 9.1] Listen. The people are talking to an estate agent.
Match the pictures of the people with the conversations.
b) Listen again. Which home should the people choose? Match
the people and the pictures of the homes.
c) What are the three most important things for each of
the people?
d) Imagine you are buying a home. What are the three most
important things for *you?*

3 Work with a partner. Imagine you are an estate agent
and a client.

a) The estate agent should interview the client. Use the words in
brackets to help you. Make notes.

1 What kind of home does the client want? (modern? small?
in the country?)
2 Ask about the type and number of rooms upstairs and
downstairs. (large kitchen / important?)
3 What would the client like outside? (want / a garage?)

b) The estate agent and the client should each write a short
advertisement for the home. Example:
WANTED: Flat near the sea, with 3 bedrooms etc.

SKILLS

Reading and speaking

1 Look at the photograph of Carol Thatcher's sitting room.

a) What do you like about the room? What do you *not* like about it?

b) What kind of person do you think lives there?

c) Name as many things in the room as you can. Example: *There's a necklace and a photo on the coffee table.*

2 Read the article. Match the paragraphs with the things in the room. Example: 1 = *A*

3 Read the article again. Are these sentences *True* (T) or *False* (F)?

1 Carol's brother is called Mark.
2 She has two nephews.
3 The cat reminds her of the cat she had when she was a child.
4 Her brother is older than she is.
5 Carol is a journalist.
6 She loved living in Australia.
7 The carpet reminds her of her mother.

4 What does this article tell us about:

1 Carol Thatcher?
2 Carol's mother, Margaret Thatcher?
3 Carol Thatcher's childhood?
4 Carol Thatcher's relationship with her brother and her parents?

5 Work with a partner. Talk about your important possessions. What do they remind you of? Example: *My desk reminds me of my first job, because I bought it with my first salary cheque.*

A I collect matches from all over the world. I have a packet from the US President's personal helicopter, but I have to hide them to stop people nicking them.

B I bought this carpet on a trip to Jordan. It reminds me of my mother. I once found her on her hands and knees straightening the fringes on a rug. I couldn't believe that someone who was running the country could find the time to worry about something so unimportant.

C I got this pot in Korea when I went to Seoul to report on the Olympic Games in 1988. The only way I could get it home was to cuddle it in my arms. When I got to the airport, I put the pot down and someone put a cigarette out in it. I was furious and shouted at him!

D I spent four and a half years in Australia working in television and newspapers and this painting of an open window frame reminds me of that time. I had finished my law degree but I didn't fancy a career in law. It was a wonderful time and I made lots of friends. When I left, the couple I was living with gave me this colourful painting. It brings back Bondi Beach on a miserable grey London day.

E These photos are of my Texan sister-in-law, her son and daughter. I like Diane a lot and am very jealous of her beautiful blond looks. I was very pleased when I heard Mark was getting married. People always expect twins to be close, but we weren't because we were both at boarding school and then we worked in different countries.

F I like this stone cat, a present from friends, because it's so life-like. I wanted pets when we were little, but everyone was always out so the house was more of a base than a home. Our parents were not good with us as children. They don't know how to talk to babies and they were both working so hard that we didn't see them very much. But they find it easier now we are adults and we have become closer.

G This cartoon was done the last Christmas that Mum was Prime Minister. Everyone was saying that she was working too hard. The cartoon shows her sitting at her desk, stirring a Christmas pudding with her foot while Dad is reading a newspaper.

(from *The Daily Mail*)

Vocabulary

Find words in the article above to complete the sentences.

1 If you c_____ something you *hold it tightly*. (paragraph C)
2 If you s_____ something you *mix it with a spoon*. (paragraph G)
3 If you feel j_____ , you *want what someone else has*. (paragraph E)
4 N_____ is an informal way of saying *steal*. (paragraph A)
5 If you are f_____ you're very *angry*. (paragraph C)

Writing

Adjectives or adverbs?

> a) A **quiet** child. (Quiet is an adjective, which describes the noun child.)
> b) He speaks **quietly**. (Quietly is an adverb of manner, which describes the verb speak.)
>
> Adverbs often, but not always, end in -ly.

1 Look at the sentences below.

a) Which of the words in italics are adverbs?
b) Which adverbs do not follow the -ly rule?

1 The film was *good*.
2 I'm not feeling *well* today.
3 He worked *hard* and passed the exam *easily*.
4 The exercise was quite *hard*.
5 Sweets are *bad* for your teeth.
6 I'm afraid I played *badly*.

2 Which is the correct word?

1 Please be *quick/quickly,* but drive *careful/carefully*.
2 What a *polite/politely* boy!
3 Do you speak English *good/well?*
4 She spoke to him very *kind/kindly*.
5 He ran down the road very *fast/fastly*.

GRAMMAR

Opinions and conditions

Will and *won't* for opinions

Look at the pictures and the box below.

I can't go out like this. Everyone will laugh at me.

Vote for us and we'll reduce unemployment.

Be careful or you'll fall off!

Relax. This won't hurt.

> a) We use *will/won't* when we think something is sure to happen in the future. This is our opinion at the time of speaking.
> b) We often use verbs like *think* or *expect* or adverbs like *maybe* or *perhaps* with *will/won't* if we are not sure about our opinions.
> I **think/expect** he'll come.   **Maybe/perhaps** he'll come.

Complete the sentences with *will* or *won't* and the verb in brackets. In 5 – 8, add a short answer.

1 Do you think it *(rain)* tomorrow?
2 I *(not be)* late tonight, I promise!
3 I expect she *(forget)* to phone, as usual.
4 There *(be)* an accident on that road one day.
5 A: I know I *(fail)* this exam.
   B: No, you _____.
6 A: Maybe he *(not go)* to the party.
   B: Yes, he _____.
7 A: Perhaps John *(help)* you.
   B: No, I'm sure he _____.
8 A: The car *(not start)* after all this rain.
   B: Yes, it _____. Don't worry!

Might or *may* for opinions

We also use the modal verbs *might* or *may*, not *will*, when we aren't sure that something will happen in the future.
I may go to Spain or I **might** stay at home. I'm not sure.

Look at the pictures of Mr Sure and Mr Unsure. They are talking about the future. What are they saying? Example:

MR SURE: *I'll pass my exams. No problem!*

MR UNSURE: *I may find a new job. I'm not sure.*

pass my exams / earn a lot of money / go out with a lot of women / not get married / have a big car

find a new job / buy a small house / get a dog / meet a nice woman / have two children

First Conditional: *if* + present + *will*

Toothfield is a town in central England which has a lot of problems. There will be a General Election soon and the candidate for the *Drongo Party* is giving a speech.

If we win, we'll reduce unemployment.

1 Look at the candidate's promise and answer these questions.

1 What verb form comes after *if?*
2 Is he talking about the present or the future?
3 Is he sure about winning?
4 Is he sure he'll reduce unemployment? Why/why not?
5 What form of the verb do we use in the 'result' clause?

It's not safe to go out on the streets at night!

A lot of our young people are homeless.

My cousin's still waiting to go into hospital but there are no beds.

There is dog dirt everywhere. It's dangerous for children to play in the parks.

There is only one bus a day and that's always late!

There are 40 people in each class and not enough books.

2 The newspaper extracts above are about some of Toothfield's other problems.

a) These are the *Drongo Party*'s answers to Toothfield's problems. Complete the sentences.

1 If we *(get in)* _____, we *(employ)* _____ more teachers.
2 If you *(elect)* _____ us, we promise we *(spend)* _____ more on transport.
3 If you *(choose)* _____ us, you have our word that we *(build)* _____ more houses.
4 We *(ban)* _____ dogs in public places if we *(win)* _____.

b) [🖭 9.2] Listen and check your answers.
c) What else do you think the candidate will say?

3 Make sentences with *if*. Start your sentences with the words in brackets. Example:
I can't go out like this. Everyone will laugh at me. *(If ...)*
If I go out like this, everyone will laugh at me.

1 Be careful or you'll fall off that wall. *(If ...)*
2 Vote for us and we'll reduce unemployment. *(If ...)*
3 Don't tease the dog! He'll bite you. *(If ...)*
4 Stop singing that stupid song. If not, I'll scream! *(I'll scream ...)*
5 Slow down or you'll have a crash. *(If ...)*

Using your grammar

1 Work in groups. How could a political party help your town? Make some notes.

a) What are the problems?
b) What could the party do to help?

2 Give your political party a name.

a) Write an election manifesto. Start like this:
Vote for the ... Party. We'll ...
b) Elect a candidate from your group to present your manifesto to the class and answer questions.

VOCABULARY

Rooms and furniture

1   Look at the picture. Write down the names of the furniture and other things in the room.

a) Work with a partner. Compare your lists.
b) Where are these things? Use the prepositions in the box.
Example: the vase of flowers
The vase of flowers is on the window sill.

next to	in	against	on top of	above	under	on

1 the bed	3 the bedside table	5 the cat
2 the wastepaper basket	4 the slippers	6 the poster

2   Make two lists of the things in the box: 1 Things for the bathroom; 2 Things for the kitchen. Some things may go in both lists. Add any other words you know.

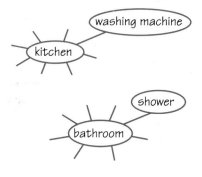

washing machine	shower	dishwasher	soap
freezer	fridge	sink	toaster	taps	bath
cupboards	cooker	towel rail	toilet	microwave
teapot	kettle	table	washbasin

Using your vocabulary

1   Work with a partner.

STUDENT A: Think of a room that you like and describe it to your partner. What are your special possessions? Where are they in the room?
STUDENT B: Try to draw what your partner is describing.

2   Then change so Student B describes and Student A draws.

USE AND REVIEW

1 Use a verb to complete these sentences. The sentences must be true about you. Then work in groups and talk about what you wrote.

1 I can't stand _____.
2 To improve my English I need _____.
3 I'm good at _____.
4 It's really boring _____.
5 Last week I forgot _____.
6 This year I have decided _____.
7 I am quite frightened of _____.
8 I hope _____ this year.
9 If I go to live abroad, I know I'll miss _____.
10 This week I have learned _____.

2 In Britain some people believe that if you break a mirror, you'll have seven years' bad luck.

a) Do you know what these pictures show?

b) Go around the class. Find out about people's superstitions. Report back to the class. Example: *Thomas believes that if a black cat crosses the road in front of you, you'll have bad luck.*

Language reference

1 *Will* + base form of verb for opinions about the future

FORM
See Unit 5, page 35.

USE
We use *will* for decisions, offers, etc.
I'll answer the phone.
We also use *will* when we feel sure that something will happen in the future.
*Everyone **will** laugh at me.* (prediction)
We'll reduce unemployment. (promise)
You'll fall. (warning)
*This **won't** hurt.* (promise)
Sometimes we add *I think, I expect, perhaps* or *maybe* when we are not sure about the future.
*I **think** they'll win the match.*

2 *Might* and *may* + base form of verb

We use *might* or *may* when we are not sure that something will happen in the future.
*It **might** rain. I'm not sure.*

3 First Conditional: *if* + present + *will*

FORM
Conditional sentences have two clauses: the '*if*' (or conditional) clause and the 'result' clause.
In the First Conditional the verb in the '*if*' clause is a present form (usually the Present Simple). This clause talks about possible future actions or events ('conditions'). The verb in the 'result' clause is a future form (usually *will, might* or *may*). Note that the *if* clause can be the first or the second clause.
If you write to me, I won't answer.
I won't answer if you write to me.
Note that there is a comma when the sentence starts with an *if* clause.

USE
We use the conditional to talk about something which must happen before something else can happen.
*I'll buy you some cigarettes (offer or promise) if you **give** me the money.* (The speaker is not sure that the other person will give the money, but the other person must give the money before the speaker will buy the cigarettes.)

•Britain and the British•

USE YOUR ENGLISH

1   How much do you know about Britain? Can you answer these questions?

1 The sport that people watch most in Britain is:
  a) cricket   b) football   c) tennis
2 The *Red Lion* is:
  a) a drink   b) a London nightclub
  c) a popular name for a pub
3 In Trafalgar Square in London you can find:
  a) Big Ben   b) Buckingham Palace   c) Nelson's Column
4 The supersonic plane Concorde is a:
  a) British and French plane   b) British and American plane
  c) British and Japanese plane
5 The capital of Northern Ireland is:
  a) Cardiff   b) Dublin   c) Belfast
6 Which of these actors is British?
  a) Meryl Streep   b) Anthony Hopkins   c) Richard Gere
7 10 Downing Street in London is/was the home of:
  a) Prince Charles   b) Sherlock Holmes and Doctor Watson
  c) the British Prime Minister
8 The population of Britain is about:
  a) 40 million   b) 60 million   c) 80 million
9 When you are driving in Britain you must carry:
  a) a driving licence   b) an identity card   c) neither of these
10 To buy alcohol in a pub you have to be:
  a) 14   b) 16   c) 18   d) 21
11 How many countries are there in the UK?
  a) two   b) three   c) four
12 If you say *Cheers* you are:
  a) having a drink   b) saying goodbye   c) saying thank you
  d) all of these
13 The most popular British newspaper is:
  a) *The Times*   b) *The Sun*   c) *Today*
14 Who was born in Stratford-on-Avon?
  a) Dickens   b) Shakespeare   c) Lady Thatcher
15 What is the traditional British Sunday lunch?
  a) roast meat   b) fish and chips   c) bacon and eggs
Check your answers on page 127.

2   Write a quiz about your country or another country.
Use reference books to help you.

a) Write questions about history, geography, sports, music,
    language, food, famous people and places.
b) Give your quiz to another student. How many questions
    can he/she answer correctly?

SKILLS

Reading, listening and speaking

The British think that they are failures at everything these days, from sport to politics. But are things so bad? We asked three foreigners what they liked about British people.

1 What do you think of the British? Choose four adjectives. You can use the words in the box.

kind	unconventional	relaxed	hardworking	funny
ambitious	friendly	creative	polite	

2 Read the interviews on the left with people who live in Britain but are not British.

a) What does each person think of the British? Use the adjectives in the box above and complete these sentences.

  1 The Russian thinks they are _____, _____ and _____.
  2 The American thinks they are _____ and _____.
  3 The South African thinks they are _____ and _____.

b) Did the three people say anything to surprise you? Are British people the same as or different from people in your country?

3 We asked two British people, a man and a woman, to describe the British.

a) [🖭 10.1 and 10.2]   Work in two groups. Group A should listen to the man. Group B should listen to the woman.

b) Look at the adjectives in Exercise 1 again. Which did your speaker agree with?

c) Work with a partner from the other group. What did you learn about British people? Use the pictures below to help you.

4 Write down six adjectives which describe a typical person from your country.

British people are very kind – that's the reason we are here. Organisations like *Amnesty International* worked really hard to get me out of the prison camp. We've lived here happily for nine years. The reason we speak good English is because the people here have been so friendly. British people are creative people, too, – just look at their gardens. This may be why there are not many British poets. They put all their creativity into their gardens.

                    (A Russian poet)

People are more relaxed here. They don't get so angry and stressed about things. In New York it doesn't matter how successful you are, you always feel you should do better. Everyone in America is ambitious – they want to be rich or important. British people aren't so conventional. They don't do what everyone else does.

      (An American magazine editor)

People are polite here. If you're driving and want to change lanes, people help you – unlike many other countries! They always say *please* and *thank you*. I love their sense of humour. They make me laugh.

      (A South African writer)

Vocabulary: idioms

The British man said, *'They can keep a completely straight face.'*

You can look up idiomatic expressions in a dictionary. First find the most important word in the sentence and then look it up in a dictionary. Here the key word is *straight*.

> **straight** /streɪt/ *adj* **1** not bent or curved: *Draw a straight line. I hate having such straight hair.* **2** level or upright: *Put the mirror straight.* **3** with no water added (used of an alcoholic drink) **4** serious: *This is his first straight play.* **5** **straight answer** an honest answer **6** **straight choice** a simple choice between two things **7** **keep a straight face** *inf* not smile or laugh even when something is funny.

Read these sentences. Match the idiomatic expressions (in **bold**) in A with the meanings in B. Use a dictionary to help you. Find the key word first. Example: 1 = c

A

1 I'm sorry I can't help. I really **haven't a clue** about it.
2 I like Margaret but she **gets on my nerves** when she's always late.
3 You look very tired. Are you still feeling **under the weather**?
4 Could you **keep an eye on** the baby while I go to the shops?
5 Tom **drives me mad** when his music is so loud.

B

a) annoys me very much
b) not well
c) have no idea
d) watch carefully
e) annoys me

Writing: organising a letter

1 The paragraphs in this letter are in the wrong order. Read the letter and answer these questions.

1 Why did Feride write this letter?

a) To give news. c) To say thank you.
b) To apologise. d) To invite.

2 Which paragraph:

a) gives news? c) gives an invitation?
b) thanks Anna for her letter? d) closes the letter?

New York
16 March

Dear Anna,

A Please write and tell me if you can come. I'm looking forward to practising my Italian and, most of all, to seeing you again.

B Life is just the same here. We have got more or less the same students in our class but we have a new teacher this term. She's nice but we have to work very hard! Everyone really misses you.

C It was great to hear from you. I'm glad the journey home wasn't too bad and that your family is well. I'm sure they were pleased to see you.

D My parents would love you to come and stay with us this summer if possible. I'm going back to Turkey in June. Why don't you come and stay with us in July? It would be great to see you again.

Best wishes to your family and love to you,

Feride

2 What is the correct order for the paragraphs? Example: the first paragraph is C.

3 Imagine you are Anna. Write a letter thanking Feride for her invitation. Accept or refuse. Use Feride's letter to help you.

Grammar

1 Question forms

Write questions in the Present, Present Perfect, Past or Future to complete this conversation.
Example: A: how / be / you?
A: *How are you?*
B: *I'm fine, thanks.*

1 A: what / do / last night?
   B: We went to the new film at the Odeon.
2 A: it / be / interesting?
   B: Yes, it was quite funny.
3 A: what / you / do / tomorrow night?
   B: I'm having a party. you / want / to come?
4 A: Yes, please. you / know / James?
   B: Yes, I do. He's a friend of my brother's.
5 A: you / invite / him / to your party?
   B: Oh, I don't know. I haven't thought about it.
6 A: you / see / him this week?
   B: Yes, I have. I saw him on Monday. Why?
7 A: I'm just interested. When / he / get back from holiday?
   B: I'm not sure. A few weeks ago, I think.
8 A: you / have / his telephone number?
   B: Yes, I have. Look, I must go. Bye.

2 Obligation

Complete these sentences with the correct form (positive or negative) of *must, have to* or *can*.

1 I'm afraid you _____ come in here if you're under 18. It's against the law.
2 I _____ remember to phone Sue. It's her birthday.
3 _____ pay our phone bill this week? Isn't it possible to pay next week?
4 You _____ take this medicine, but you'll feel better if you do.
5 You _____ smoke in the corridors but not in the classrooms.
6 I've told you a hundred times! You _____ cross the road without looking. You'll have an accident.

3 Mixed verb forms

Put the verb in brackets in the correct form: Present, Past, Present Perfect, Future, Conditional, *-ing* or *to*.

Joe *(just arrive)* (1) *has just arrived* in Britain from Chile and he *(stay)* (2) _____ here for a year. He needs *(improve)* (3) _____ his English because he *(study)* (4) _____ it at university next year. At the moment he *(live)* (5) _____ in London but he is thinking of *(go)* (6) _____ to study in York. People *(tell)* (7) _____ him that it's a good place to go because there *(not be)* (8) _____ many foreigners. He *(never go)* (9) _____ there. The problem is that if he *(go)* (10) _____ to live in York, it *(cost)* (11) _____ a lot of money to visit London. He would like *(come)* (12) _____ back often. Joe is happy *(be)* (13) _____ in Britain but he is sure he *(miss)* (14) _____ his family.

4 Quantity

Which is the correct answer? Example:
A: Have you got a / *any* butter? B: Yes, but not *much* / many.

1 A: You've got *some* / *any* money, I hope.
   B: A *little* / *A few.*
2 A: I don't have *much* / *many* soap.
   B: I'll give you *a little* / *a few.*
3 A: Could I borrow *some* / *any* coffee?
   B: Yes, how *much* / *many* do you want?

Pronunciation

Weak forms and contractions

a) [🔊 10.3] Listen. How many words are there in each sentence? A contracted form *(he's)* is two words.

1 _____ shop?   3 _____ walk _____?
2 _____ coffee?   4 _____ lunch _____.

b) Listen again and complete the sentences.

Vocabulary

1 Non-idiomatic phrasal verbs

In English we often use a preposition or an adverb after a verb. We call these expressions *phrasal verbs*. We can often understand the meaning from the two parts. Complete these sentences with a preposition or adverb from the box. Sometimes there is more than one possibility.

on down over in up away round off

1 If you're feeling ill, why don't you go and lie _____ on the bed?
2 When she was running out of the house she fell _____ the cat.
3 He turned _____ the radio and went to sleep.
4 Put _____ a jumper if you're cold.
5 Pick _____ that paper from the floor.
6 She turned _____ to see who was following her.
7 It started to rain so they went _____ the house.
8 I gave the book _____ as a present.

2 Idiomatic phrasal verbs

We can't always understand the meaning of phrasal verbs from the two parts. We call these idiomatic phrasal verbs.

break down	give up	take after	try on
pick up	hang on	get on with	rub out

a) Match each phrasal verb with a picture on the right.
b) Work with a partner. Write a short sentence about each picture.
c) Work in groups. Compare your sentences.

3 Noughts and crosses

Work in groups of three.

STUDENT A: Look at page 128 for the questions.
STUDENT B: You are the X (cross).
STUDENT C: You are the 0 (nought).

Who begins? Throw a coin or a dice to decide. The person who begins chooses a square. Student A asks a question. If the answer is correct, mark the square with X or 0. Student A then asks the other person a question, and so on. The winner is the first person with a line of 0s or Xs. Check your answers on page 130.

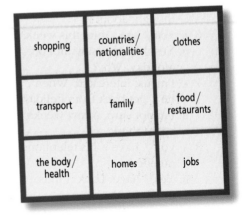

shopping	countries/nationalities	clothes
transport	family	food/restaurants
the body/health	homes	jobs

Use your English

Work with a partner. What would you say in these situations?
Use the words in brackets to help you. Take turns to be A and B.

1 A: *(Ask the waiter to bring you a black coffee.)*
  B: _____ .
2 A: I'm sorry I'm late.
  B: _____ .
3 A: George, I'd like you to meet Mr Potter.
  B: _____ .
4 A: *(Ask for the bill in a restaurant.)*
  B: _____ .
5 A: *(Ask for 10 first class stamps.)*
  B: _____ .
6 A: *(Invite your partner out.)*
  B: *(Accept.)*
  A: *(Suggest where to meet and give a date and time.)*
  B: *(Offer to pick A up.)*
7 A: *(Invite your partner, informally, to go somewhere.)*
  B: *(Make an excuse.)*
8 A: *(Answer the phone.)*
  B: *(Ask to speak to C.)*
  A: *(Ask B to wait.)*

Writing

This is part of a letter which a student sent to his teacher. Rewrite
the letter. Correct the underlined mistakes. Add any words which
are missing (✐ means something is missing).

> I went home last _thursday_ ✐ _my_ flight was twelve hours ✐
> _but_ I felt very tired when I arrived. While I was _comeing_
> out of _the_ airport I saw my family. My family were waiting
> for me and it was _nice_ to see _my family._ I _liked_ eating the
> _brazilian_ food again. We went yesterday to the beach.
> I often think of our school and all the fun I had
> at the school. Is the class working _good_ ✐ I will continue
> studying _the_ english _and_ I really want to speak it _good._

Use a different word

Don't repeat 'my family'!

Word order

Don't repeat 'school'!

LEARNING REVIEW

1 Which area/s do you think you are best at and worst at?

a) Put them in order 1– 6 (1 = best, 6 = worst).

- Grammar
- Reading
- Listening
- Speaking (including pronunciation)
- Writing
- Vocabulary

b) Which particular language areas would you like to revise? For example, *the Present Perfect*, or *the vocabulary of clothes*.

c) Which general skills areas would you like to do more work on? For example: *Writing*.

2 Work in groups. Talk about what you can do outside the classroom to improve your English. Think about:

a) good ideas for improving your vocabulary. For example, listening to English or American songs, keeping a vocabulary notebook.

b) ways of improving your grammar. For example, revising the *Language reference* pages.

c) ways of improving your reading and listening.

•Enjoying life•

USE YOUR ENGLISH

Filling in a form

1 When do you have to fill in a form?

2 When would you fill in these forms?

See the World Holidays

HOLIDAY BOOKING FORM · WINTER

NAME

DEPARTURE AIRPORT

Application for Employment

Education

Previous experience

IMMIGRATION FORM

Please complete in BLOCK CAPITALS

Surname

First names

Address in the UK

Date of birth

Nationality

Present occupation

Length of stay

Purpose of visit

Passport number

Signature

For official use only

RENTACAR

Booking form

Driving licence number

Additional driver/s

---

3 Work with a partner.

a) These are the answers to questions about some of the headings on the immigration form. What are the headings?

b) Make questions for the answers. Example:
How long are you staying in this country?

c) [▱ 11.1] Listen. Sally Jones has just arrived at Heathrow Airport in London. She's going through Immigration. Compare the Immigration Officer's questions with your questions.

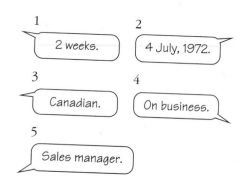

1 2 weeks.

2 4 July, 1972.

3 Canadian.

4 On business.

5 Sales manager.

4 Work with a partner. He/She has come to England to study English for three months. Ask your partner questions and fill in the form in Exercise 2 for him/her.

SKILLS

Listening and speaking

1   Philip does a lot of deep-sea diving. Look at the picture. What do you think happened to him?

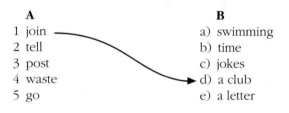

2 [📼 11.2]   Listen to Philip.

a) Were your guesses correct? Philip had a lucky escape. How?
b) Look at the pictures on the left. Which one does Philip **not** talk about?
c) Listen again. Complete the sentences with one or more words.

rock climbing

camping

Philip and Sarah's lives are very _____. Once, in the Gulf of Mexico, they were _____ the bottom of the sea when Sarah _____ a shark. When she _____ her arms at Phil he thought she _____ breathe. When Phil realised what the problem was he moved _____ but the shark _____ interested and swam _____ him.

3   Find the /ʃ/ sound on the phonemic chart on page 132.

a) Which letters make the /ʃ/ sound in the word *parachuting*?
b) [📼 11.3]   Listen to these words. Which letters make the /ʃ/ sound: information, especially, profession, finish, machine?
c) Practise saying the words. Stress the correct syllable.

flying a plane

4   Philip says: '*We don't spend our free time **doing crosswords**.*' Match the verbs from A with the nouns from B.

A	B
1 join	a) swimming
2 tell	b) time
3 post	c) jokes
4 waste	d) a club
5 go	e) a letter

Writing: spelling

[📼 11.4]   Listen to ten sentences. Write the word you hear at the end of each sentence.

parachuting

GRAMMAR

Comparatives and superlatives

1 The dream of many animal lovers is to go on safari. Look at the pictures above and answer the questions. Answers on page 129.

1 Which is faster, a leopard or a cheetah?
2 Which is more short-sighted, a rhino or a tiger?
3 Which has better hearing, a snake or a giraffe?
4 Which is heavier, an elephant or a giraffe?
5 Which animal has a longer neck, a giraffe or an ostrich?

2 Which words are the adjectives in these sentences?

1 A rhino is more short-sighted than a tiger.
2 A cheetah is faster than a leopard.
3 An elephant is heavier than a giraffe.

Comparative adjectives

When we compare two things we use the comparative form of adjectives.

a) Adjectives of one syllable: adjective + -er.
   Example: nice → nic**er** (than)
b) Adjectives of two syllables ending in -y:
   adjective + -ier. Example: pretty → prett**ier** (than)
c) Adjectives with two, three or more syllables:
   more + adjective. Example: interesting →
   more interesting (than)

3 Match the grammar rules a)–c) with 1–3 in Exercise 2.

4 Compare the animals in the picture. Use adjectives from the box and any other adjectives you know. Example:
A cheetah is smaller than a tiger.

small	attractive	slow	noisy	ugly
nice	beautiful	strong	dangerous	

Superlative adjectives

When we compare three or more things we use the superlative form of adjectives.

a) Adjectives of one syllable: adjective + -est.
   Example: slow → (the) slow**est**
b) Adjectives of two syllables ending in -y:
   adjective + -iest. Example: noisy → (the) nois**iest**
c) Adjectives with two, three or more syllables: most +
   adjective. Example: beautiful → (the) **most** beautiful

5 In your opinion which of the animals is:

1 the nicest?   3 the most dangerous?
2 the ugliest?   4 the best swimmer?

6 What are the comparative and superlative forms of these adjectives?

	Comparative	Superlative
1 good	_____	the _____
2 bad	_____	the _____
3 hot	_____	the _____

Check your guesses in the *Language reference* on page 71.

Making comparisons

> When we make comparisons we can also use:
> a) *as* + adjective + *as*. Example:
>   *She's **as** old **as** I am* (we are the same age).
> b) *Not as* + adjective + *as*. Example:
>   *She isn't **as** old **as** I am* (we are not the same age).

7 Use *as ... as* and *not as ... as* to make comparisons.
Example: towns / cities *(big)*
Towns aren't as big as cities.

1 milk / ice-cream *(fattening)*
2 reading a novel / watching a film on TV *(enjoyable)*
3 spiders / snakes *(horrible)*
4 men / women *(emotional)*

8 [💾 11.5] Listen and disagree with these sentences.
Example:
A: Spring's wetter than autumn.
B: *No, spring isn't as wet as autumn.*

9 Complete these sentences. Use the comparative or superlative form of the adjective in brackets or *(not) as ... as.*

1 Hang-gliding is *more exciting than* reading a book. *(exciting)*
2 I weigh over 100 kilos. You're _____ me! *(light)*
3 I think jazz is _____ rock music. *(good)*
4 The necklace wasn't _____ I thought. *(expensive)*
5 You look _____ you did yesterday. *(bad)*
6 What's _____ month of the year? *(wet)*
7 My _____ holiday was in Cuba. *(enjoyable)*
8 Is cheese _____ meat? *(healthy)*
9 Schooldays are _____ days of your life! *(good)*

Using your grammar

1 Compare the following. Use comparative and superlative forms. Examples: walking, jogging, running
Running is harder than jogging.
Walking is more relaxing than running.
Jogging every morning is the best thing for your health.

1 living in a flat, living in an hotel, living in a house
2 playing cards, skiing, sleeping
3 learning a foreign language, learning to ride a horse, learning to cook
4 going shopping, visiting museums, going to a disco
5 travelling by train, travelling by plane, travelling by car

2 Compare these people. Use the words in the box. Example:
Anne is tidier than Bill.

Bill   Anne

Susan and Alan   Jeff and Joan

> friendly   funny   hard-working   quiet   polite
> good-looking   young   tidy   sociable   old-fashioned

3 Work in groups. Compare the people in your class.

a) Give yourself a mark from 1 to 5 for the following:
tall (1 = not tall; 5 = very tall), fit, old, tidy, hard-working.
b) Who is:

1 the tallest? 3 the oldest? 5 the most untidy?
2 the fittest? 4 the tidiest? 6 the most hard-working?

VOCABULARY

Hobbies

1 Work with a partner. Here are some things you can do in your free time. Match words from A and B.

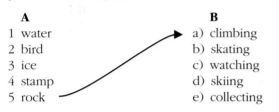

A	**B**
1 water	a) climbing
2 bird	b) skating
3 ice	c) watching
4 stamp	d) skiing
5 rock	e) collecting

2 Look at the pictures on the right.

a) Think of a hobby for each picture.
b) What other hobbies do you know?
c) Which hobby is the most:

- enjoyable?
- exciting?
- expensive?
- dangerous?
- unusual?
- relaxing?
- energetic?
- popular?

3 What do we call the people who do these things?

HOBBY	PERSON
dancing	_'dancer_
cycling	_____
photography	_____
cooking	_____
music	_____
acting	_____

Mark the stressed syllable in each word.

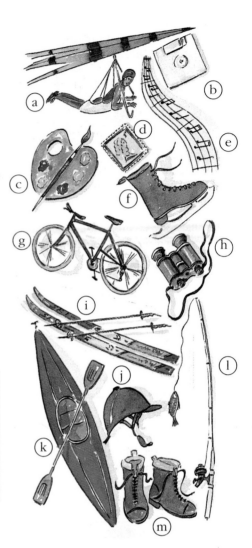

Using your vocabulary

1 What do you like doing in your free time? Use expressions like: _I'm quite keen on / I like / I enjoy walking._

2 Prepare a short talk about hobbies. Choose a hobby from Exercises 1–3 above which you would like to try. Then choose a hobby you would not like to try. Give your reasons. Make notes.

3 Work in groups. Give your talk to the group.

USE AND REVIEW

1   Antonio has just arrived in Britain. What should he say in these situations? Use the words in brackets. Example: he wants to buy a pair of trousers. (try on / pay by cheque?)
Could I try these trousers on ? Can I pay by cheque?

He wants to:
1 book a table at a restaurant. *(reserve a table by the window / 4 people / 6 o'clock?)*
2 order food at a restaurant. *(chicken and salad / red wine?)*
3 pay the bill at a restaurant. *(bill / take Visa / service included?)*
4 start a conversation with a young woman at a disco. *(here / often?)*
5 invite a friend to the cinema. *(fancy?)*
6 invite someone he doesn't know very well to the cinema. *(like?)*

2   Where would Antonio hear these expressions? Match the expressions in A with the places in B.

A	**B**
1 Day return, please.	a) in a baker's
2 Three second class stamps, please.	b) at a railway station
3 How would you like your money?	c) in a post office
4 I'd like a small white loaf, please	d) in a bank

3   What other things can you tell Antonio about Britain? Example: *when the British say 'Cheers'* or *when the British shake hands.*

4   Work with a partner. Antonio wants to visit *your* country. What should he say and do there?

Language reference

1 Comparatives

FORM

For adjectives which end with one vowel followed by one consonant, double the consonant in the comparative form.
*hot → hot**ter** (than)*
Note the irregular forms.
*good → **better** (than)*
*bad → **worse** (than)*

USE

We use comparatives when we compare two things.
*A train is fast**er** than a bus.*

2 Superlatives

FORM

a) For adjectives of one syllable, add -est at the end in the superlative form.
   *young→ the young**est***
b) For adjectives which end in one vowel + one consonant, double the consonant and add -est at the end.
   *hot → the hot**test***
   Note the irregular forms:
   *good → the **best***
   *bad → the **worst***

USE

We use superlatives when we compare three or more things.
*April is the wet**test** month of the year.*

3 *as* + adjective + *as*

When we make comparisons we can also use *as* + adjective + *as* (which means the same or equal) or *not as* + adjective + *as* (which means not the same or not equal).
*My hands are **as** cold **as** ice.* (My hands are cold. Ice is cold. My hands are like ice.)
*He's not **as** strong **as** I am.* (We are not equal. I am stronger. He is weaker.)

•Witness•

USE YOUR ENGLISH

Making conversation

1   These people are at a party.
a) [🖭 12.1]   Listen and match the conversations with the couples.
b) Listen again and complete these sentences from each conversation.
  1 I'm _____ now, _____ . How _____ ?
  2 You're _____.
  3 I _____ think _____. I haven't seen him.
  4 I _____. We're playing football later.
c) In some of the conversations the people are pleased to see each other. In which conversations? How do you know?

2   Answer these questions about Conversation 4.
1 Is it going to snow? What does the woman think?
2 Does the man want snow? Why/Why not?

3   What would you say in these situations?
Which is the correct answer?
1 A: Do you think it'll be hot tomorrow?
  B: *I hope so. / I hope not.* We're on holiday.
2 A: Have we got any milk in the fridge?
  B: *I think so. / I don't think so.* I bought three bottles yesterday.

4   Work with a partner.
a) Complete each conversation with one of these expressions.

I hope so.   I don't think so.   I think so.   I hope not.

1 A: Let's go for a picnic.
  B: Do you think it's going to stay sunny?
  A: Yes, _____. The weather looks very good.
2 A: Hurry up!
  B: Have we missed the train?
  A: _____. It's the last one today.
3 A: It's freezing in this room.
  B: Is there a heater?
  A: _____. I can't find one.
4 A: I passed all my exams.
  B: Well done! Are you going to university?
  A: _____. I want to go very much.
b) Practise each conversation.

Missing

YESTERDAY PAT WENT BACK to her normal job as a policewoman. But for a year she was close, very close, to a man who told her he had killed his
5 wife. Keith Brown didn't know Pat was a policewoman. And he fell in love with her.

So what happened? In the summer of 1992 Brown and his wife had a
10 furious argument. The neighbours heard everything. After that day no one saw his wife again. The police were sure Keith Brown had killed her but he refused to answer any
15 questions.

Early in October, Brown answered a lonely-hearts advertisement in the Sun Valley Times. The woman who put the advertisement in the news-
20 paper telephoned the police. She told them about Keith Brown's letter to her. The police decided that police-woman Pat, not the woman, should meet Keith Brown. Pat phoned Keith
25 Brown – the first of many telephone conversations about life and love, and about his wife.

They had their first meeting in a pub in Preston. The police could listen to
30 Brown's conversation with Pat because she had a small microphone inside her dress. Brown and Pat met five more times and he fell in love with her. On February 25, 1993,
35 Brown asked her to live with him. She said: "I can't live with you. Your wife might come home at any time." Pat wanted to end their relationship.

But she agreed to meet Brown once
40 more. While they were talking, Brown suddenly confessed. He told Pat, "My wife will never come home again. I killed her. Voices in my head told me to kill her. I'm sorry. I love you. I want
45 to spend my life with you." Again, the police recorded everything. They arrested Brown.

But the judge did not accept Brown's confession as evidence.
50 Although Brown confessed that he had killed his wife, he went free.

And Pat? She has moved to another job.

SKILLS

Reading and speaking

YOUNG WOMAN with good sense of humour looking for serious loving relationship with single man. Reply Box no. 5467

1 Look at the pictures above. They tell the story of Keith Brown and a woman called Pat. Match the sentences with the pictures.
1 The *lonely-hearts advertisement* which Keith Brown read.
2 The police are *arresting* Keith Brown.
3 Keith Brown is *confessing* that he *killed* his wife.
4 Pat is going to *record* Keith Brown's words on her *microphone*.
5 The *judge* is listening to the *evidence*.

2 What do you think happened?

3 Read the article on the left and check your answers.

4 Read the article again. Are these sentences *True* (T) or *False* (F)?
1 The police found the body of Brown's wife in the summer.
2 Brown said his wife left him.
3 Pat put a lonely-hearts advertisement in the newspaper.
4 Pat and Brown first met in a pub.
5 Pat had a secret microphone.
6 Pat said to Brown, 'Keith, I want to live with you.'
7 The judge sent Brown to prison.

5 Do you agree with these sentences? Why/Why not?
1 The judge was wrong not to accept the evidence.
2 What the police did to catch Keith Brown was a good idea.
3 I could do what Pat did.

Vocabulary

Look at these nouns from the article on page 73: *conver'sation, 'meeting, ad'vertisement.*
Make the verbs in the box into nouns with one of these endings: *-ation, -ing, -ment.* Example: *improvement.*

improve	feel	argue
examine	save	explain
pronounce	warn	

Writing: *the*

> The woman put an advertisement in **the** Sun Valley Times.
>
> We use **the** when we know there is only one:
> **the** Times   **the** sun
> **the** President   **the** Pacific
> **the** Eiffel Tower **the** River Nile
> **the** National Gallery
> **the** United Nations
>
> We do not use **the** before:
> • continents (*Africa*)
> • most countries (*France, Brazil, Indonesia,* but *the USA, the UK*)
> • languages (*Spanish*)
> • mountains (*Mount Everest, Mont Blanc* but *the Alps, the Himalayas*)
> • towns (*Preston*)
> • street names (*Oxford Street*)
> • stations and airports (*Heathrow*)
> • meals (*I've had breakfast*)

Cross out *the* in these conversations where necessary.
1 A: Have you been to ~~the~~ Italy?
  B: Yes. It's the only country in the Europe I would like to live in. I also speak the Italian.
2 A: What's the name of the place you're moving to?
  B: The Oldham.
  A: Oh, I was born there.
  B: We've bought a house in the Park Road near the river.

GRAMMAR

The Second Conditional

Jane is filling in a questionnaire in a magazine. Read the first part of the questionnaire and her answers.

ARE YOU HONEST?

1 Imagine you find £20 sticking out of a cash machine. Would you give it to the bank?

If I found £20 sticking out of a cash machine, I would keep it. I wouldn't give it to the bank.

2 Imagine you find someone's personal diary. Would you read it?

Yes, if I found someone's personal diary, I'd read it.

Monday

I had a wonderful time with Joe this evening.

He really is great.

1 Look at Jane's answer to question 1 again.
1 Has Jane found £20 or is she imagining it?
2 Is she talking about the past, the present or the future?
3 What verb form is *found*?
4 Compare Jane's answer with this sentence:
  If I find £20, I'll keep it.
  In which sentence does Jane think it is possible that she will find £20?

2 Read Jane's answers to questions 1 and 2 again and complete this rule.
In the Second Conditional, the *if* part of the sentence often has the _____ form of the verb. In the other part of the sentence, the base form of the verb follows _____.

3   Jane didn't finish her answers to questions 3 and 4 of the questionnaire.
Complete her answers with the correct form of the verb. Use *would, wouldn't* or *'d* where necessary.

3   Imagine a friend asks your opinion about the clothes he/she is wearing. You think he/she looks terrible. Would you tell him/her?

No, if a friend (ask) _____ me my opinion about the clothes he was wearing, I (not, say) _____ he looked terrible. I (lie) _____.

4   Imagine you book into an expensive hotel. There is a wonderful towel in your bathroom. Would you steal it?

If I (book)_____ into an expensive hotel and there (be) _____ a wonderful towel in the bathroom, I (not, steal) _____ it. I (leave)_____ it.

4   Work with a partner. Are you honest? Ask and answer the questions in the questionnaire.

Using your grammar

1   Work with a partner. How would you spend your perfect weekend? Ask each other questions. Example: Where /go?
Where would you go?
1 Who /go with?
2 How /get there?
3 Where /stay?
4 What /have to eat and drink?
5 What /like to do?
6 Who /send a postcard to?

2   Work with a partner. What would you do, think or feel in these situations? Example: Your house is on fire.
If my house was on fire, I'd phone the fire station. I'd be very upset.
1 You are a famous person.
2 You meet the US President in the street.
3 You win a million dollars in a competition.
4 You can have any job you like.
5 You have to change your name.
6 You can live where you like.

I'd like to be a woman because I'd like to have a child.

I'd like to be a man because you can get a better job.

3   If you had your life again, would you prefer to be a man or a woman? Tell your partner and give your reasons.

4   Work in two groups.
GROUP A
Write the questions for a quiz. Use the Second Conditional.
1 What kind of music /you sing /you be Pavarotti?
2 Which city /you go to /you want to visit the Vatican?
3 What languages /you speak /you live in Singapore?
4 Where /you be /you be at Harvard?
GROUP B
Write questions for a quiz. Use the Second Conditional.
1 Which sport /you play /you be at Wimbledon?
2 What you see /you visit the Louvre?
3 Where you be /you be at Copacabana?
4 What you do /you have a balalaika?
Now Group A asks Group B questions and Group B asks Group A questions. The group with the most correct answers wins. (See page 126.)

VOCABULARY

Crime

1 [💾 12.2]   Listen.
a) Match the stories with the pictures.

b) Which word goes with which picture?
   burglar   robber   thief

2   Complete the table. Use a dictionary to help you. Mark the stressed syllable in each word.

PERSON	VERB	CRIME
burglar	¹*burgle*	_____
thief	–	_____
robber	_____	_____

3   Complete the sentences. Use one of the words above.
1 Someone _____ their house while they were on holiday.
2 They planned to _____ a bank.
3 The problem of car _____ is getting worse.

4   Complete these sentences with the correct form of the words in the box.

prison   arrest   steal   commit   thief

Police Constable Roberts heard the sound of footsteps. He went quietly into the house. Roberts hoped to _____ the burglar while he was _____ the crime. As Roberts got to the stairs, he jumped on the man. Roberts was horrified to see that the man was the judge who last week sent a _____ to _____ for six months because he _____ a box of chocolates.

5   Work in groups. Put the pictures on the right in the correct order. Write the story. Start like this:
First, he broke a window and ...

USE AND REVIEW

Helen

Steven

Rebecca

Mark

1   Work with a partner.
STUDENT A
Look at page 129.
STUDENT B
Look at the picture above. You are going to ask your partner five questions about the people.
First write your questions. Example:
Is Sandra taller than Helen?
a) Show your partner your picture. Ask him /her your questions.
b) Compare the people in the two pictures. Example:
I think Helen is the most attractive.

2   Choose one of the people in your picture.
a) Which hobby do you think he/she does?
b) Imagine you are the person in the picture. Tell your partner about your hobby. Why do you like it? Don't say who you are.
c) Your partner must guess who you are.

Language reference

1 Would

FORM

Positive
I /You /We /He /She /They **'d (would)**   like to be rich.
Negative
I /You /We / He /She /They   **wouldn't (would not)**   like to be rich.
Question
Would   I /you /we /he /she /they   like to be rich?

USE

a) for requests (***Would*** *you like a drink?*)
b) to express a wish (*I**'d** like to go to the cinema.*)
c) when we imagine situations that are not likely to happen (*I**'d** spend my perfect holiday on a luxury ship.*)

2 The Second Conditional

FORM

If + past form, *would* (*'d*) + base form of verb

Positive
If I **found** £20, I **would keep** it.
Negative
If I **found** £20, I **wouldn't keep** it.   If I **didn't speak** French, I **wouldn't understand**.
Question
If you **found** £20, **would** you **keep** it?   What **would** you **do** if you **found** £20?
Short answer
If you **found** £20, **would** you **keep** it?   Yes, I **would**. /No, I **wouldn't**.

There is usually a comma after the *if*-clause and before the main clause (*If I thought he looked terrible,* I would ...)
The *if* part of the sentence can come second and then there isn't a comma before *if*.
   *I wouldn't tell him **if** I thought he looked terrible.*

USE

We use the Second Conditional when we imagine situations that are unlikely or impossible in the present or the future.
   If I found £20 ... (But I haven't and it is unlikely.)
   If I were you ... (But I'm not. It's impossible.)
We use past verb forms after *if* to show that a situation is imaginary. We are not talking about past time.

•Love is all around•

USE YOUR ENGLISH

Finding the way

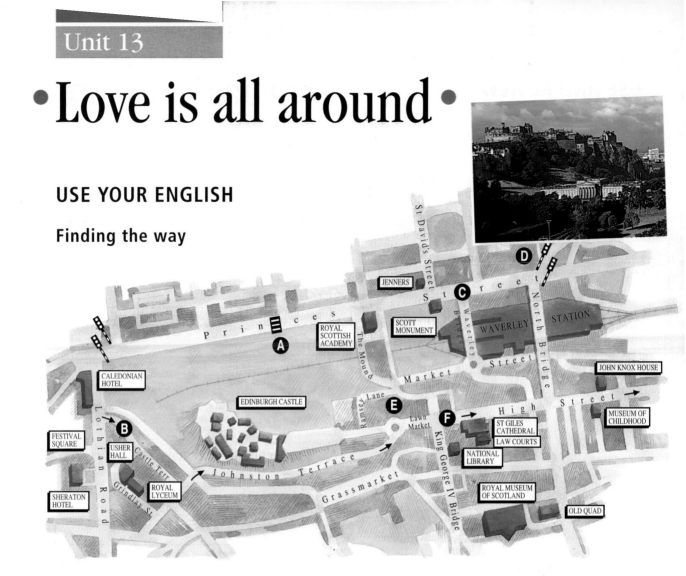

1   Look at this map of Central Edinburgh.

a) Can you find:

1 some traffic lights	4 a crossroads
2 a T-junction	5 a one-way street
3 a pedestrian crossing	6 a roundabout

b) Where are they? Match A with B.

A

1 The Museum of Childhood
2 Waverley Station
3 Jenners
4 St Giles Cathedral
5 The Old Quad
6 The Law Courts

B

a) on the corner of Princes Street and St David's Street
b) behind St Giles Cathedral
c) opposite John Knox House
d) next to the Royal Museum of Scotland
e) between Waverley Bridge and North Bridge
f) in front of the Law Courts

2 [▭ 13.1]   Penny has invited Carl to a concert. She is giving him directions on the telephone.

a) Listen and follow Penny's directions on the map. Where is the concert hall?

b) Listen again and complete these sentences.

1 Turn _____ and _____ until you get to Princes Street.
2 _____ and walk _____ Princes Street for about fifteen minutes.
3 Go _____ the Royal Scottish Academy.
4 You'll see the Castle and the Mound _____.
5 When you get to the end of Princes Street, _____ again _____ Lothian Road.
6 Walk _____ Lothian Road.

3   Work with a partner. Choose a place on the map of Edinburgh. Don't tell your partner the name of the place. Give your partner directions from Waverley Station.

SKILLS

Listening

1   Read the words on the right. They are of part of a song called 'Love is all around'. The words in italics are wrong.

a) Replace the wrong words with one of the words in the box.

toes	love	feel	come on	everywhere

b) [📼 13.2]   Listen and check your answers.

1   I *hear* it in my fingers
     I *hear* it in my *nose*.
     Well, love is all around me
     and so the feeling grows.
5   It's written on the wind,
     It's *nowhere* I go.
     So if you really *hate* me
     Go away and let it show.

2 [📼 13.3]   Listen and complete the song.

3   Answer these questions.

1 Is he sure she loves him?
2 What do you think they promised?

      You know I love you,
10   I _____ will.
      My mind's made up
      By the way that I _____.
      There's no beginning,
      There'll be no _____
15   'Cos on my love, you can
          depend.

      I see your face before me,
      As I lay on my _____.
      I kind of get to thinking,
20   Of all the things you _____.
      You gave your promise to me,
      And I gave mine to _____.
      I need someone beside me,
      In everything I _____.

4   Which words rhyme with these words? Example: grows (line 4) *toes.*

go (line 6), depend (line 16), bed (line 18), you (line 22)

Reading and speaking

1   What does the word 'romantic' mean to you?

2   Read this extract from a survey on monogamy and answer the questions.

1 Some people think that staying married is very difficult. Who think this, younger people or older people?
2 Is it better to be romantic or unromantic if you want to stay married?

3   Work with a partner. Read about these people's ideas and answer the questions.

> You can't be romantic these days. Everybody is too busy working.

> We make sure we have a romantic holiday on a boat every year.

1 What different ways are there of being romantic?
2 Is it important for young people and old people to be romantic? Why/Why not?
3 What advice would you give to a couple who have been married for fifteen years and who want to be romantic?

Last week we interviewed 1000 people for our survey on monogamy. One in five people said, 'Monogamy is
5 unnatural.' A quarter of the people said, 'Monogamy was all right twenty years ago but now it's old-fashioned.' And it wasn't the younger people who said that but
10 those in their late twenties and older. They've tried to be together 'for always'. But for a lot of them it didn't work.
    Nearly three-quarters of the
15 people dreamed about marriage when they were children. They dreamt that they would marry and live with the same person for the rest of their lives. But often the
20 most romantic people have broken marriages. And those who are most happily married generally didn't have dreams about their future when they were children.

(from *New Woman*)

Writing: reference words

1   What do the words in italics below refer to in the article on monogamy on page 79?

1 but now *it's* old-fashioned. (line 7)
2 the younger people who said *that* ... (line 9)
3 But for a lot of *them* it didn't work. (line 12)
4 T*hose* who are most happily ... (line 21)

2   Complete these sentences. Do not repeat words from the first sentence.

1 I like French films. I like *them* a lot.
2 A: What do you think of *Hamlet*?
   B: I've never seen _____.
3 I like those jeans over there. They're better than _____ you're wearing.
4 A: Pam's just got married.
   B: Who told you _____?
5 A: I saw Jim today.
   B: Where did you see _____?
6 A: A woman called for you today.
   B: What was _____ name?

GRAMMAR

Defining relative clauses: *who, which, that, where*

1   Tick (✓) the boxes you agree with and add sentences of your own.

Likes and dislikes

· ·

1 **What kind of people do you like?**

a) I like people who (that)
   show their feelings ☐   laugh a lot ☐   give a lot of presents ☐
   I like people _____

b) I am jealous of people who (that)
   can eat anything and stay slim ☐   always look wonderful ☐
   understand computers ☐
   I am jealous of people _____

c) I don't like people who (that)
   hurt animals ☐   drive badly ☐   eat garlic ☐
   I don't like people _____

2 **What kind of things do you like?**
(Examples: cars, animals, films)

I like trains which (that) run on time. ☐
I don't like dogs which (that) bark a lot. ☐
I like/don't like _____

3 **What kind of places do you like?**
(Examples: hotels, airports)

I like shops where the assistants are polite. ☐
I don't like restaurants where they play music. ☐
I like/don't like _____

2   When we want to add information and make it clear which person, thing or place we are talking about we use:

1 _____ (or *that*) for people.   3 _____ for places.
2 _____ (or *that*) for things.

Complete these sentences with *who, which, that,* or *where.*

1 Have you been back to the town _____ you were born?
2 She's the kind of person _____ likes to go to parties.
3 Who took the bag _____ was on the table?
4 A vegetarian is someone _____ doesn't eat meat.
5 That is the horse _____ won the race.

Using your grammar

1 Work in groups. Ask each other the questions from the questionnaire. Example:
Do you like people who show their feelings?

Write down the answers. Report back to the class.

2 Complete these sentences

1 The perfect parent is someone who ...
2 My ideal room is a place where ...
3 Computers are things which ...
4 A good host is someone who ...

3 These are meanings of some difficult words from units 1–12. Is each sentence *True* (T) or *False* (F)?

1 A chemist's is a place where you buy books.
2 A cardigan is like a jacket which keeps you warm.
3 A greengrocer is someone who sells stamps.
4 10 Downing Street is the place where the President of the USA lives.
5 A model is someone who wears new clothes at shows.
6 A platform is a place where you get on a plane.
7 A shoplifter is someone who builds houses.
8 Slippers are shoes which people wear in the house.

Adjectives: word order

1 Read these sentences.
I like men with large, round, brown eyes who wear nice clothes.
A wallet is a small, flat, leather case for paper money.

SIZE	SHAPE	COLOUR	MATERIAL
large	round	brown	
small	flat		leather

2 Put the adjective in brackets in the correct place. Example:
a square box (wooden)   *a square wooden box*

1 a long woollen scarf (grey)
2 a pointed thing (large)
3 a dark road (long)
4 a big cat (white)

(We) use a ... for ...-ing

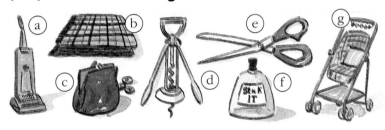

1 Match the words with the pictures.

1 a vacuum cleaner
2 a buggy
3 a corkscrew
4 scissors
5 glue
6 a blanket
7 a purse

2 What do we use the things in Exercise 1 for? Example:
*We **use** a vacuum cleaner for cleaning carpets.*

Using your grammar

Work with a partner. Describe one of the things below to your partner. He/She must guess which thing you are describing.

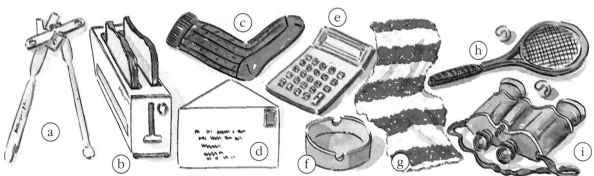

VOCABULARY

Describing people

(a) (b) (c) (d)

1 [■ 13.4]   Listen. Four people are trying to find their friends.

a) Match the pictures of the friends with the conversations.

b) Listen again. Write the expressions which describe the friends. Make two lists: 1 Expressions with *is* (*He / She **is** quite tall*); 2 Expressions with *has (got)* (*He / She **has (got)** long, black hair*).

c) Add more expressions to each list. Example: opposites like *short blond hair*.

d) In these sentences, the words in *italics* are not appropriate. Replace the word in *italics* with one of the words in brackets.

   1 She's lovely and *skinny.* (bony, slim)
   2 Rob's a very *pretty* man. (handsome, beautiful)
   3 Lucy is very *high.* (tall, great) She's not *middle-height.* (medium, average height)

The correct words are in the conversations in Exercise 1a). Listen again and check.

2   We can use the adjectives in the box on the right to describe people's personalities. Make three lists: 1 Good; 2 Bad; 3 Not

Add other words to each list.

lazy	clever	tidy
sociable	bad-tempered	
lively	patient	mean
cheerful	talkative	shy

Relationships

Read Matthew's letter to an old friend who lives in the USA. They haven't seen each other for many years. Complete the sentences with the correct form of the verbs in the box. Use a dictionary to help you.

go out together	fall in love
get married	be fond of
get divorced	get pregnant

I _____ Laura at school but I didn't really fancy her until we met at a dance several years later. The next day I took her to the cinema. That was the day we first kissed and _____. It was very romantic. We _____ for about a year before we _____ and decided to have a baby. Soon afterwards Laura _____ and we had a baby boy we called James. We both adored him. Unfortunately that was the beginning of our problems. We argued about everything. Two years later we _____ but we've stayed good friends. We still see each other every week and take James out together.

Using your vocabulary

Read the two lists on the right.

a) Imagine **your** ideal partner. Make two similar lists.

b) Work with a partner. Compare your lists.

I want someone who
• is kind
• wears nice clothes
• has got blue eyes
I don't want someone who
• is bad-tempered
• has a very long beard

USE AND REVIEW

1   Read this extract from a magazine article. Why was Suzanne brave?

Suzanne Daniel, a hospital secretary, was out shopping last week. She was walking along the street when a shop assistant screamed. A thief ran out of a shop with a heavy cash register.
Suzanne and the thief came face to face. She tried to stop the thief but he pushed past her. Then she ran after him down the street and tried to stop him getting into his car. Furious, the thief threw the cash register at her and ran away.

2   What would you do in these situations? Use the ideas in brackets.

1 You are walking down a street and you see a thief running out of a shop with a cash register. (*If I saw ...,   try to stop / run away / phone the police / do nothing*)
2 You see someone shoplifting. (*tell assistant / speak to the person / do nothing*)
3 You hear someone in your house in the night. (*phone police / get a gun / hide*)
4 You see smoke coming from inside a house. (*phone fire station / go and look*)

3   Complete these sentences.

1 You would go to prison in my country if ...
2 If I had 10 children, ...
3 You would feel better if ...
4 If I couldn't sleep for three days, ...
5 Would you give me a kiss if ...?

4   What nouns, verbs or adjectives do you associate with *police, kill* and *steal?* There are example words in the box. Add more words.

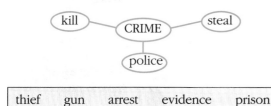

| thief | gun | arrest | evidence | prison |

Language reference

1 Defining relative clauses

Who, which, that, where are relative pronouns. We use them to link ideas, add information and make it clear which person, thing or place we are talking about.

a) *who* or *that*

We use *who* (or sometimes *that*) for a person or people.
    *I like people **who (that)** listen.*
    *I don't like people **who (that)** talk all the time.*
    *She is the doctor **who (that)** lives next door.*

b) *which* or *that*

We use *which* or *that* for things.
    *I'm talking about a car **which (that)** uses very little petrol.*

c) *where*

We use *where* for places.
    *A library is a place **where** you borrow books.*

Note that there is no comma before a defining relative clause.

2 Adjectives: word order

(See page 81.)

3 *(We) use a ... for ...-ing*

    *What do you **use** this **for?***
    *I **use** it **for** clean**ing** the carpet.*

•A real fan•

I've just won the competition!

USE YOUR ENGLISH

Saying the right thing

1 Work with a partner. What would you say in answer to the people on the right? Choose the best answer, a), b) or c).

1 a) Good luck! b) Hard luck! c) Well done!
2 a) Oh! What a pity! b) I don't care. c) Not at all, don't mention it.
3 a) Yes, it's all right. b) Sorry! c) That's a good idea.
4 a) That's no good. b) Oh, I **am** sorry! c) Better luck next time.

I'm sorry I can't come to your party.

2 Complete these conversations.

a) Choose the best answer, a), b) or c).

1 PAM: Hi, Sue. Guess what? PAM: I'm having a baby in July.
  SUE: What?   SUE: Oh, _____.

  a) Well done! b) Congratulations! c) It'll be all right.

2 SHOP ASSISTANT ONE: I'll get one for you. I won't be a second.
  RICHARD: That's OK.
  SHOP ASSISTANT TWO: Can I help you?
  RICHARD: _____.

  a) No, I'm being served, thanks. b) Yes, I hope so.
  c) Certainly.

Quiet!

b) [🔲 14.1] Listen and check your answers.

3 Work with a partner. You have been at a friend's house for the weekend. These sentences are from your conversation on Sunday evening.

a) Put the conversation in the correct order.

- Well, it's time to go. We've had a great time. Thanks for everything. ☑
- Sure. Bye. Look after yourself. ☐
- Next time you must come to us. ☐
- Yes, we'd love to. Have a safe journey. Don't forget to write. ☐
- Not at all. We've enjoyed having you here. ☐

My brother's not well.

b) [🔲 14.2] Listen and check your answers.

SKILLS

Reading

People who 'follow' famous people are called 'fans'. Read these articles on the right about two fans, Saf and Ruth. Saf is a fan of George Michael. Ruth is a fan of Barbra Streisand.

a) Work with a partner and answer these questions.

1 Saf is obsessed (he thinks about the singer most of the time). How do you know?

2 How do you know Ruth is obsessed?

3 How are Saf and Ruth different?

b) Work in two groups.

GROUP A

Read the article about Saf again and write questions for these answers. Example:
He owns a newsagent's shop.
What does Saf do?

1 CDs and copies of George's suits.

2 In January.

3 Ten years ago.

4 On TV.

GROUP B

Read the article about Ruth again and write questions for these answers. Example:
She is going to hear Barbra sing.
What is Ruth going to do next week?

1 Three months ago.

2 Thousands and thousands of pounds.

3 Yes, she feels she is an old friend now.

4 A lot.

c) Work with a partner from the other group. Check your partner's questions.

I'm a real fan

SAF SATHI, 25, is known as 'George' in the newsagent's shop he owns in Kent, because of his obsession with the singer George
5 Michael.

Saf spends his life trying to be better than George Michael's other fans. He earns £400 a week. Out of this £400 he buys every
10 new Michael CD (at £12 each) and copies of George Michael's suits (at £300 each). His wife, Savita, is expecting a baby in January: he would like to name it
'Michael' if it's a boy. 15

'I've got all his albums on tape and CD. I know exactly what he's doing. I don't miss a thing,' Saf says.

Saf's obsession started about 20 ten years ago when George Michael was in the pop group *Wham!* 'He's so smart. His clothes, his look, the way he is different from the others.' 25

Saf's dream is to be George Michael. Already well-known for copying his idol, he is now trying to get work on TV as a George Michael lookalike. 30

Next week Ruth Davison will spend 10 per cent of her annual salary. She is
35 going to hear Barbra Streisand sing. Miss Davison, an office clerk, has bought seats for all four of Barbra Streisand's concerts in London, at £260 a
40 ticket.

However, that is not as much as she spent on flying to Las Vegas to see Streisand's $1,000-a-ticket show three months
45 ago. It is also not as much as she spent on a Beverly Hills show that she flew to California for. It was there that Miss Davison, 32, met and spoke to Streisand.
50 'I said I'd come all the way from England. She said "Oh, good," and smiled nicely. That made it worth the money.'

Most of Streisand's fans are
55 not rich. Many, like Miss Davison, are prepared to spend all their savings to see one of the last superstars in the world.

'I can't think of anything I
60 would rather spend my money

on,' says Miss Davison. 'I've spent thousands and thousands of pounds over the years. Any spare money I've got goes on Barbra. No one else can sing 65 like her. It touches you deep inside and makes you want to get to know her. I feel I know her well now. I feel she is an old friend. 70

'I can feel her feelings. I believe she worries a lot and I don't think she's very confident. But she's done a lot for women. She has made it 75 possible for women to become film directors. She was one of the very first.'

(from *The Daily Telegraph* and *The Independent on Sunday*)

Vocabulary

1 Match the words from the articles about Saf and Ruth in A with their meanings in B.

A	B
1 miss (line 18)	a) *adj* for one year
2 annual (line 34)	b) *adj* sure of yourself
3 spare (line 64)	c) *v* fail to get
4 confident (line 74)	d) *adj* extra

2 Complete these sentences with the correct form of one of the words from Exercise 1.

1 I'm nervous. I don't feel very _____.
2 What's your _____ salary?
3 Have you got a _____ pen I could borrow?
4 We arrived at the station late and _____ the train.

Writing

Adverbials in sentences

> a) Adverbials of manner come after the object or after the verb if there is no object.
> *Barbra smiled at her **nicely**.*
> b) Adverbials of time usually come at the end or sometimes at the beginning of a sentence.
> *He came to see me **last week**.*
> ***Last week** he came to see me.*
> c) Adverbials of place usually go at the end of a sentence.
> *We walked slowly **into town**.*
> d) See page 17 for frequency adverbs.

Put these words in order.

1 speaks / he / English / well
2 quickly / ran / road / he / the / down
3 early / went / she / bed / night / last / to
4 her / to / listens / always / he / carefully

GRAMMAR

Used to

1 The writer Margaret Forster is talking about being fifty.

I haven't changed my idea of a good time very much over the years. I used to enjoy staying in with a new novel and a really good apple, and now I enjoy staying in with a new novel and a glass of wine.

I used to behave very badly in my twenties. I remember once I screamed in the middle of Oxford Street and all the cars suddenly stopped. In my thirties I was too tired to find the energy to scream.

It used to be very difficult to write. I wanted to be a mother, a writer and a wife and do everything myself. Now I can write all day if I want to.

(from *Male and Femail*)

1 When Margaret stayed at home in the past, what did she do?
2 When she stays at home now, what does she do?
3 What was she like in her twenties and her thirties?
4 Did she often use to scream in the middle of Oxford Street?
5 Was it difficult for her to write in the past?
6 Is it difficult for her to write now?

2 Look at the *Language reference* on page 89 for information about *used to*.

a) Complete these sentences with the Past Simple or *used to*. In one sentence both verb forms are possible. Which one?

1 Yesterday morning I *(have)* _____ toast for breakfast.
2 When I was young I *(like)* _____ toast.

b) Complete these sentences with *used to* and the base form of a verb.

1 I _____ out a lot but now I stay in more.
2 When Tony was younger he _____ sweets but he doesn't like them now.
3 Megan _____ in France but now she lives in Wales.
4 Children _____ books but now they play computer games.

3 [▭ 14.3] Listen to these sentences and mark the stressed words. Example: *We 'used to 'swim in the 'sea*.

1 I used to wear short skirts.
2 He used to drive fast cars.
3 We used to listen to the radio.
4 I used to be very unhappy.
5 She used to eat meat but now she's a vegetarian.

4   Make sentences with *used to* from these pictures and words. Example:
People used to travel by boat but now they travel by plane.

1 I/live Rio/Paris   2 Pete/poor/rich   3 Angie/ride/drive

Question tags

1   Read about tonight's TV programmes. What would you like to watch?

6.00 WILDLIFE ON ONE
(repeat) Elephants in India.

6.30 FILM: STAR TREK V: THE FINAL FRONTIER
(1989) Vulcan kidnaps three people. A Klingon warship goes to help. Stars William Shatner.

8.10 PANORAMA
A day in the life of a nurse in modern Britain.

9.00 NEWS & WEATHER

9.30 HEADHUNTERS
New drama in the world of big business. Stars James Fox and Francesca Annis.

10.20 RORY BREMNER
Successful comedian gives his ideas about love.

11.00 LATER WITH JOOLS HOLLAND
Chat and music with Sting and reggae from Sly and Robbie.

2 [🖭 14.4]   Nikki and Tom are talking about tonight's TV.

a) Listen. Which programmes does Nikki like? Which programmes does Tom like?
b) Complete the sentences.

1 He's a good actor, _____?
2 It wasn't very good last week, _____?
3 You still like Sting, _____?
4 We've seen it, _____?
5 You liked him last time, _____?
6 Let's watch that, _____?

c) [🖭 14.5]   Listen and check your answers. Look at the *Language reference* on page 89 for information about question tags.

Using your grammar

Used to

Work with a partner. Tell him/her about the changes in your life over the years. Talk about things like:

- daily routine
- hobbies
- clothes
- personality
- travel
- likes/dislikes
- sports
- food

Question tags

Work with a partner. Find out about Keanu Reeves.

STUDENT A
Look at page 127.

STUDENT B
Read this article.

KEANU REEVES

was born in Beirut in 1965. His mother is English and his father is Chinese-Hawaiian. When he was young he wanted to be a racing driver. Keanu began acting when he was 18. He has played in the films *Dracula* and *Much Ado About Nothing*. Keanu loves riding motorbikes. He has got a 1974 Norton.

You and your partner both have information about Keanu Reeves. Most of the information is the same, but you've got some information which your partner hasn't got. Use question tags to check and find the extra information. Example:
A: *He was born in 1965, wasn't he?*
B: *Yes, he was.*

VOCABULARY

Ententainment

1 We use these things in home entertainment. Match the words in the box with the pictures.

video recorder	CDs	loudspeaker	cassette
video tapes	batteries	TV screen	headphones
stereo system	microphone		

2 We use the words in the box for other kinds of entertainment.

exhibition	screen	interval	performance
front row	audience	to book	stage	to clap
sculpture	to buy a programme	drawing	

Make three lists with the words in the box for: 1 A pop concert; 2 An art gallery; 3 A cinema. Use a dictionary to help you.

3 Where would you hear these sentences? Match the sentences in A with the places in B.

A
1 'I like it when the clowns throw water at each other.'
2 'It's so cruel! I hate to see the animals locked up.'
3 'Everything here is so old, Dad!'
4 'How much money have you lost?'

B
a) a museum
b) a casino
c) a circus
d) a zoo

4 Look at the puzzle. Find the word for someone who:

1 acts (*a* _____)
2 plays funny parts on TV or in a film (*c* _____)
3 directs a play or a film (*d* _____)
4 plays a musical instrument in public (*m* _____)
5 directs an orchestra (*c* _____)
6 writes a book (*a* _____)
7 creates works of art (*a* _____)
8 writes music (*c* _____)

```
F L G U A D K I A T J
C O N D U C T O R P G
D F A C T O R Z T Y J
I M V B H J E S I P L
R F P C O M P O S E R
E P W N R T Z X T Y M
C U Y C O M E D I A N
T O W Q A Z V F H J L
O M U S I C I A N R W
R T W A O G F D K J U
```

Using your vocabulary

Work with a partner. Talk about something you have watched, heard or read recently. Use some of the adjectives from the box. Ask and answer questions like:

What was the title? Who directed, sang or wrote it? What was it about? What was your opinion of it?

interesting	exciting	amusing	boring	relaxing
shocking	frightening	depressing		

USE AND REVIEW

1   Work in groups. Complete these sentences with *who*, *which* or *where* and give the answer. The group with all the correct answers wins.
Example:
A person who paints pictures is a painter.

1 The place _____ you catch a train is a _____.
2 A person _____ looks after sick people in hospital is a _____.
3 A thing _____ you imagine when you are asleep is a _____.
4 A person _____ cuts your hair is a _____.
5 A long thin animal without legs _____ eats other animals is a _____.
6 A place _____ you buy medicine is a _____.
7 A person _____ writes for a newspaper is a _____.

2   Work with a partner.

STUDENT A
Look at page 130.

a)   STUDENT B
You and your partner have similar pictures. Ask questions and find ten differences. Don't look at your partner's picture and don't show him/her your picture.

b) Now look at your partner's picture and answer these questions.

1 What does the woman look like?
2 What kind of person do you think she is?
3 Where is she?
4 What is happening in the picture?

Language reference

1 *Used to*

FORM
Used to + base form of the verb

Positive and negative			
I /You /We They /He /She	**used to** **didn't use to**	**like** **drive**	wine. fast cars.
Question			
Did you **use to smoke?**		Yes, I **did**. /No, I **didn't**.	
How many cigarettes **did** you **use to smoke?**			

USE

Used to can express a past situation which has finished or changed.
> I **used to like** jazz but now I like rock.
> I **used to go** to jazz clubs every week.

We do not need to use a time expression with *used to*. In the above examples we can also use the Past Simple with a time expression.
> I **liked** jazz **when I was younger** but now I like rock.
> I **went** to jazz clubs **when I was at college**.

We cannot use *used to* when something happened only once:
> I went to a rock concert last night. (NOT ~~used to go~~)

2 Question tags

FORM
Positive sentence + negative tag.
> They**'re** happy, **aren't they**?

Negative sentence + positive tag.
> She **isn't** right, **is she**?

In sentences with *is/ are* or with an auxiliary *doesn't/ don't, have/ has, can/ should* we make the tag with *is/ are* or the auxiliary.
> There**'s** nothing left, **is** there?
> Peter **doesn't** like you, **does** he?
> She **hasn't** finished, **has** she?

In sentences without an auxiliary we make the tag with *do/ does/ did*.
> He likes you, **doesn't** he?
> You went to New York, **didn't** you?

Note there are two exceptions.
> I**'m** late, **aren't** I?
> **Let's** go out, **shall** we?

USE

We use question tags when we think the other person agrees with us or we want the other person to agree with us. Our voices usually go down at the end of question tags.

•School rules•

USE YOUR ENGLISH

Changing money

1   Carlos is a student. He has just arrived from Argentina for a week's holiday in Britain. What has he got in his wallet?

1 How much sterling can you see?
2 How can he get sterling when he has no more cash?

2   Carlos is changing a traveller's cheque at a bank.

a) Read this conversation and complete the sentences.

BANK CLERK: Yes, sir?
CARLOS: Can I _____ a traveller's cheque for $100?
BANK CLERK: Sure. _____ at the top, please. Can I see your passport?
CARLOS: What's the _____ rate at the moment?
BANK CLERK: $1.41 to the pound. So that's £70. How would you _____ the money?
CARLOS: Three twenties and a ten, please.

b) [📼 15.1]   Listen and check your answers.
c) Work with a partner and practise the conversation.

3   Work with a partner. Look at the list of £ exchange rates. Change the sums of money below (cash or traveller's cheques) into sterling. Take turns to be the bank clerk and the customer.

- seventy five Cyprus pounds
- one thousand five hundred Japanese yen
- three hundred Swiss francs
- 500 Austrian schillings
- two hundred Brazilian reals

4   Look at the pictures. Carlos is buying a coat in a shop.

a) What do you think Carlos and the shop assistant are saying?
b) Write a conversation beginning:

CARLOS: How much ... ?

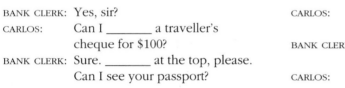

Tourist rates

Austrian schilling	16.40
Brazilian real	1.36
Cyprus pound	0.73
French franc	7.96
German mark	2.35
Greek drachma	358.00
Italian lire	2755.00
Japanese yen	156.93
Spanish peseta	194.00
Swiss franc	1.97
US dollar	1.41

SKILLS

Reading and speaking

Work with a partner. Read about a school in England and answer the questions.

1 What are the differences between this school and your school?
2 What is/was a school day like in your school? (Example: *The day started at ...*)
3 Think about schools in your country. Make a list of rules (Example: *You have to wear a uniform. No fighting.*) and punishments (Example: *Staying after school.*)

THE KING'S SCHOOL, ELY

The school day begins at 8.50 am. Children have to be at school by 8.40 am and the day ends at 4.00 pm. There are classes on Saturdays.

All pupils have lunch at school.

All children have to wear school uniform in the day time. The uniform is simple and inexpensive.

Listening and speaking

1 Look at the photos. Guess which school has more rules.

2 [15.2] Karen, from the USA, and Rie, from Japan, are fifteen. At the moment they are at the King's School in Ely, England. Listen to them talking about schools in their countries. In which country do the pupils spend more time at school?

3 Work in groups.

[15.3] GROUP A, listen to Karen.

[15.4] GROUP B, listen to Rie.

Look at the list on the right. What rules and punishments do you hear?

4 Work with a partner from the other group.

a) Compare your information. Answer these questions.

1 Which school has more rules?
2 What do students in the American school do when their teachers ask them to stay in the classroom at lunchtime?
3 How do Karen's and Rie's schools in their countries compare with their school in England?
4 What is the difference between modern and traditional school uniforms in Japan?

b) Ask your partner about his/her school. Use these words to help you: *like school? memories? your first day? how old? good / bad things about schools in your country?*

RULES
She has to
• wear a school uniform
• study very hard
She mustn't
• take drugs
• wear her school uniform to town
• smoke
• fight
• wear a hat
In her school she can
• talk in class
• do what she likes
• wear what she likes
• not go to classes

PUNISHMENTS
The teachers sometimes
• call the police (*the cops*)
• ask students to stay after school
• phone the pupils' parents

Vocabulary

Karen uses the informal word *cops* to talk about 'the police'. Match the informal words in italics with the words in the box. Use a dictionary to help you.

employer	very good
want	wait	children

1 I'm taking the *kids* to the zoo.
2 Do you *fancy* a drink?
3 *Hang on* a minute.
4 He asked his *boss* for more money.
5 We're *great* friends.

Writing: linking words

> Note where the linking words come in a sentence.
>
> **CONTRAST**
> a) *School finishes at 4* **but** *we can't go home until 7.* (middle)
> b) **Although** *school finishes at 4, we can't go home until 7.*
>   *We can't go home until 7,* **although** *school finishes at 4.* (beginning or middle)
> c) *School finishes at 4.* **However**, *we can't go home until 7.* (beginning)
>
> **ADDITION**
> a) *Karen goes to school in England. Rie goes to school in England,* **too**. (end)
> b) *Karen goes to school in England. Rie* **also** *goes to school in England. (She is* **also** *studying in England.)* (before the main verb but after verbs like *be, have, can*)

Join these sentences with linking words. Change the order of the words if necessary.

1 The actors were very good. I didn't like the film very much.
2 I'll buy this bag. I'll buy these shoes.
3 My car is old. It runs very well.

GRAMMAR

Quantity

Mrs Todd

Some-, any-, no-, every- words

1 Mrs Todd is talking about modern life.

a) Look at the words in italics. Which one do you think is correct?

'These days *everyone/someone* is very busy. There's not enough time for *something/anything*. *Someone/No one* stops to talk to you. I hate it.'

b) [▭ 15.5] Listen and check your answers.
c) Which correct answer in a) means:
 • no people?
 • all people?
d) In negative sentences do we use *something* or *anything*? (See page 41 for the difference between *some* and *any*.)

2 Complete the sentences. Use one of the words in the box:

PEOPLE			THINGS		
some-/any- no/every-	+	one	some-/any- no-/every-	+	thing

1 I've got <u>something</u> for you. I hope you like it.
2 Please close your eyes. I don't want _____ to look.
3 There's _____ in the box. It's empty.
4 There's _____ at home. Where have they gone? _____'s out.
5 I can't do _____ right. _____ I say is wrong.
6 I've never met _____ as intelligent as you.
7 There's _____ on the phone for you.
8 The office is empty. Where is _____?

Sarah

Mr Parsons

Too and very

> It's **very** warm today. It's great. Let's go out.
> It's **too** warm today to go out. Let's stay in.
>
> Too means 'more than is good'.

3 Mr Parsons is talking about modern houses.

a) Complete his sentences with *too* or *very* .

'I like modern houses. I moved into one last year. It's _____ nice. I didn't like my old house. It was _____ big for me. The one I live in now is _____ small but it's just right for me. I'm _____ old to live in a big house.'

b) [🖸 15.6] Listen and check your answers.

4 Make sentences about these pictures using *too*.

cold/swimming   2 tired/go out   3 ill/get up   4 expensive/buy

5 Join these sentences using *very* or *too*.

1 He is young. He can't get married.
2 It's dark. You can't see the road.
3 This programme is interesting. It is interesting for children.
4 My coffee is hot. I can't drink it.

Too much and too many

6 Read these sentences.

*I ate too **much** food last night. I feel ill this morning. There are too **many** students in the class. One of them is going to another class.*

Match the words in the box with *too much* or *too many*. (See page 41, for the difference between *much* and *many*.)

> people   time   houses
> salt   trees   money

7 Sarah is talking about how she relaxes.

a) Complete her sentences with *too much* or *too many*.

'Everyone works very hard these days. During the week I can't relax. I have _____ to do. So on Saturdays I like to find something to read and take a long deep bath. I might watch TV but these days I think there are _____ game shows on. I don't like them.'

b) [🖸 15.7] Listen and check your answers.

8 Make sentences using *too much* or *too many*. Example: Sorry / can't come. People to see.
I'm sorry I can't come. I've got too many people to see.

1 Can't buy / house. Costs / money.
2 You've got / furniture / clothes. Sell some.
3 Can't see. People in front of me.
4 Spend / time watching TV.
5 Can't eat this cake. Sugar.

VOCABULARY

Education

1 Look at the pictures on the right.

a) Match the school subjects with the pictures.

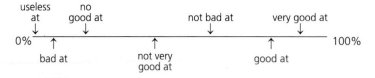

| languages   science   art   IT (information technology) |

b) Make a list of other school subjects. Examples: *maths, history.*

c) Which subjects are/were you:

useless
at
no
good at
not bad at
very good at
↓   ↓   ↓   ↓
0% ↑   ↑   ↑   100%
bad at   not very   good at
good at

d) Which subjects do/did you enjoy most?

2 The verbs in the box often go with the nouns in italics. Complete the sentences with the correct form of the verbs. Sometimes more than one answer is possible.

| pass   get   attend   do   fail   have   take   go   study |

1 Let's _____ *a break*!
2 Please _____ your *homework*.
3 How many *exams* are you _____? I hope you don't _____ any. You must _____ for them if you want to _____ them all.
4 Have you _____ *a degree*?
5 Do you want to _____ *to university?*
6 Do you _____ *lessons* on Saturdays?
7 We have to _____ *classes* every day except Sunday.

Using your vocabulary

1 Work in groups. Which sentences do you agree with? Why? Number the sentences 1 to 8. (1 = you agree with this sentence the most.)

1 Schools should teach more practical subjects. (Examples: *cooking, typing.*)
2 Music and art should be extra classes.
3 There shouldn't be sports in school time.
4 There shouldn't be school uniforms.
5 Parents should help in the school.
6 We should have our education when we are adults, not when we are children.
7 Parents should educate their children at home.
8 You learn more from going to work than going to university.

2 Compare these ideas. Which help you to learn best?
Example: *You learn more from your parents than from television.*

• books   • your friends   • television   • working   • school   • parents

USE AND REVIEW

1   There is one mistake in each sentence.
Can you correct the mistakes?

1 Carly used to go to a Thai restaurant last night.
2 These days, I used to catch the bus at six o'clock every morning.
3 When he was younger he used to spending every Saturday in bed.
4 You haven't seen her, haven't you?
5 David likes tennis, likes he?

2   Can you do this crossword puzzle?

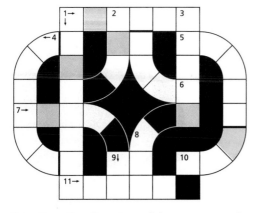

a) Follow the direction of the arrows and write answers. Use a dictionary if necessary.

1 → Somebody who writes books.
1 ↓ The people who watch a pop concert.
2 ↓ The in_____val in the middle of the concert lasts thirty minutes.
3 ↓ A: Let's go out.   B: All _____ then.
4 ← It happens every year. The event is _____.
5 → Let's go to the c_____ and have a good time. I always like the elephants.
6 ← A: Can I speak to Julie?
    B: _____ on a moment.
7 → A m_____m is a place where the public can look at interesting objects.
8 ↓ I am a big _____ of the Manchester United football team.
9 ↓ Leonardo da Vinci was a great _____tist.
10 → We took the children to the _____ to see the monkeys.
11 → She _____ £20,000 a year.

b) Put the letters in blue in the correct order to find an important grammar point (two words).

Language reference

1 *Some-*, *any-*, *no-*, *every-* words

FORM

The words *some, any, no* and *every* can join with the words *-one* and *-thing. (someone, everything).*

USE

We use the words *someone, anyone, no one, everyone* for people *(one = person).* We use the words *something, anything, nothing, everything* for things.

a) *Some-* words *(someone, something)*
Positive
    *I want you to meet **someone.***
Offers and requests
    *Would you like **something** to drink?*
    *Could I have **something** to eat?*

b) *Any-* words *(anyone, anything)*
    Questions
    *Did you see **anyone**?*
    Negatives
    *I haven't done **anything** today.*

c) *No-* words *(no one, nothing)*
no one = no person
    *There's **no one** at home. They're all out.*
nothing = no thing
    *There's **nothing** in the room. It's empty.*

d) *Every-* words *(everyone, everything)*
everyone = all people
    ***Everyone**'s out. There's no one at home.*
everything = all things
    *The shop sells **everything** you need.*

2 *Very* or *too?*

too = more than is good, right or necessary.
    *It's **very** late. We must go.*
    *It's **too** late. We have missed the last bus.*
    *This coffee is **too** hot to drink.*

3 *Too much* or *too many?*

too much/too many = more (in quantity) than necessary
too much = before uncountable nouns.
    *We have **too much** milk.*
    *There's **too much** to do.*
too many = before countable nouns.
    *We have **too many** books.*
    *There are **too many** people.*

•Have you heard the news?•

USE YOUR ENGLISH

Saying sorry

1   What has happened in the photographs on the right?

a) In each of the pictures what does the other person say next?
Choose one of these:

1 I'm awfully sorry. I didn't see you there.
2 Sorry. I had a very important business meeting.
3 I'm very sorry. I haven't got any more.
4 Sorry, but my watch stopped.

b) What does the first person answer? Choose one of these:

1 It doesn't matter. It's not your fault.
2 Oh, yes. You always say that.
3 That's all right. Don't worry.
4 I don't believe you.

c) [🖭 16.1]   Listen. Were your guesses correct?

> Where have you been?

> For heaven's sake. Look what you are doing!

2 [🖭 16.2]   The British use
the word 'Sorry!' in many other
situations. Listen to this
conversation on the London
Underground then put the
pictures in the correct order.
Listen again and complete the
sentences.

1 ANDY: You didn't ——
   me last night.
   NICOLA : —— ?
2 Oh, ——. Are you trying
   to —— —— ?
3 —— but this is —— ——
   date.

3   Work with a partner. Make conversations for these situations.
Use 'sorry' where necessary.

1

STUDENT A
You've broken a glass in a
restaurant. Tell the waiter.

STUDENT B
You are the waiter. Be polite.

2

STUDENT A
Invite B to a party.

STUDENT B
Refuse politely and give
a reason.

3

STUDENT A
Tell B you are cold.

STUDENT B
You can't hear what A is
saying. Ask him/her to repeat.

SKILLS

Reading and speaking

1   These pictures show two different newspaper stories. Which three pictures tell a story about a man who eats light bulbs and razor blades? What do you think the other story is about?

2   Work in two groups.

a) GROUP A: Read 'Call me Mother'.
GROUP B: Read 'Jim's dangerous life'.

b) Which of these sentences are *not* correct?

GROUP A

1   The old lady ...
a) arrived at the restaurant with the couple.
b) said the woman looked like her daughter.
c) hoped the woman would meet her daughter.
d) wanted the couple to pay for her.

2   The couple ...
a) wanted to talk to the old lady.
b) felt sorry for the old lady.
c) thought the lady was telling the truth.
d) asked why the lady's meal was not on the bill.

GROUP B

1   Jim Rose isn't paid for his work.
2   The police asked him to do a show.
3   The police thought he was drunk.
4   His mouth was full of wine.
5   Jim only eats one light bulb a day.
6   He ate a light bulb for a radio programme.
7   It hurt him immediately.
8   The doctors were angry when they found glass inside him.

3   Work with a partner from the other group. Tell your story in your own words. Use the pictures in Exercise 1 and the answers from Exercise 2.

CALL ME MOTHER

A friend and her husband were enjoying a romantic evening at an expensive restaurant when they saw an elderly
5 lady. She was sitting all alone looking in their direction. They smiled back politely and the old lady went across to their table. 'I'm sorry to trouble you,' she began, trying not to
10 cry, 'but you look like my daughter. She was killed last year and I do miss her terribly. I wonder if you would do something very kind for me?' The couple said yes.
15 'It would make me very happy if, just as I'm leaving, you would say, "Goodbye mum", and wave to me.'

'Certainly,' the couple replied. How could they possibly refuse? A few minutes later the old lady stood 20 up to leave so the couple waved and said 'goodbye' as 'mum' walked out.

Then the couple asked for their bill. But after checking and rechecking, they called the manager because 25 they thought the total was wrong.

'This £25 is for your mother's meal,' the manager told them. 'Before she left she said that her daughter would pay.' 30

Jim's dangerous life

It was not a good week for Jim Rose, an unusual man who eats razor blades and light bulbs and breathes fire for a living.
5   On Monday Rose was driving from London to Amsterdam when he was stopped by police and breathalysed. Rose does not drink alcohol. However, he had put so much
10 alcohol in his mouth when he was breathing fire that the breathalyser almost blew up. He had to pay £250.

Then for a radio programme, Rose ate a light bulb (his fifth that day), part of which 'went down the wrong 15 way'. A friend explained: 'There is a right way and a wrong way to eat a light bulb. Jim did it wrong.' Although he felt nothing immediately, he became ill the next 20 day. Doctors were angry when they found that he was full of broken glass.

(from *The Guardian* and *The Daily Telegraph*)

Vocabulary: negatives

We use *un-*, *in-*, *dis-*, *non-* to make negatives.
Example:
*Jim Rose is an **un**usual man.*

a) Which word in each of these pairs is correct?
Use a dictionary to help you.

1 unhappy	inhappy
2 insense	nonsense
3 disagree	unagree
4 nonluckily	unluckily
5 unhonest	dishonest
6 nonstop	unstop
7 incorrect	discorrect
8 nonkind	unkind

b) Mark the stressed syllable in each correct
word. Example: *un'happy.*

Writing: improving a paragraph

Last night Fred was very unhappy. Fred decided
to go to a ✐ restaurant. Fred went alone. Fred
didn't want to go with the ✐ people who were
staying with Fred. Fred was very tired. Fred had
an argument with a ✐ waiter. Fred decided to go
home. Fred wanted to drive ✐ all the way. Fred
nearly fell asleep. Fred decided to stop. ✐ some
policemen saw Fred. The policemen asked Fred
what Fred was doing. Fred was angry. Fred
shouted at the policemen. The policemen
were angry. The policemen took Fred to the
police station.

Read the paragraph above.

a) Add one of the words in the box below in the
places marked ✐. You may have to change
a → an. Use each word once.

nonstop	unfriendly	inexpensive
unluckily	unpleasant	

b) Join the 16 sentences together to make 7–8
sentences. Use the words in the box below.

and	but	because	so	however	too

c) Do not repeat words again and again.
Use the words in the box below.

he	they	him	them

GRAMMAR

The passive

1 Read this extract from a newspaper article
and answer the questions.

Swedish youth stopped

The youth was stopped from working as an au pair
in Britain because he is male. He was
questioned at Heathrow airport when he arrived
and then

1 Are we more interested in the young man
or the people who stopped him?
2 Do we know the names of the people at
Heathrow airport who questioned him?
Are they important?

2 Look at these sentences and answer
the questions.

	SUBJECT	ACTIVE VERB	OBJECT
a)	*They*	*questioned*	*the youth*

	SUBJECT	PASSIVE VERB
b)	*The youth*	*was questioned.*

In which sentence:

1 is the word *questioned* in the Past Simple?
2 is the word *questioned* a past participle?
3 did the subject do something to the object?
4 did someone (we don't know who) do
something to the subject?

3 Look at the box below and complete the
sentences.

The passive is formed with *be* + the past participle.			
I	**am / was**		
You / We / They	**are / were**	**taken**	to the police.
He / She / It	**is / was**		

ACTIVE
1 Someone stole my gloves yesterday.
PASSIVE
_____ yesterday.

ACTIVE
2 Someone hit Pat last night.
PASSIVE
_____ last night.

4 Find an example of the passive in the story on the right.

> With the passive we use *by* when we say who or what did something to the subject.

The postman was attacked by a dog while he was delivering letters. The animal bit his hand. The postman ran shouting for help while the dog was chasing him.

5 What is the passive form of these verbs?

1 give	it *is given*	(PRESENT)
2 eat	they _____	(PRESENT)
3 meet	she _____	(PAST)
4 drink	it _____	(PAST)
5 build	it _____	(PAST)
6 make	they _____	(PRESENT)
7 sell	it _____	(PAST)

6 Complete these sentences with the correct form of the passive. The first two are done for you.

1 They were found in a forest.
  Where *were they found?* (question)
2 He was met at the airport.
  He *wasn't met at the airport.* (negative)

3 She's called Tania.
  What _____ ? (question)
4 We were given the right tickets.
  We _____ . (negative)

7 Complete these sentences with the correct form of the verb in brackets. Use the active or passive of the Past Simple.

1 The best-selling game *Monopoly (create)* _____ in the 1930s. In 1975 more Monopoly money *(print)* _____ in the USA than real money.
2 In the film *The Gold Rush* Charlie Chaplin *(eat)* _____ his boots. They *(make)* _____ of black sugar.
3 In 1985 part of Mexico City *(destroy)* _____ by an earthquake. Over 2,000 people *(kill)* _____ , but rescue workers *(find)* _____ over fifty newborn babies alive under a building.
4 In March 1944 Sergeant Alkemade's plane *(hit)* _____ by a gunshot and he *(jump)* _____ 5,485 metres without a parachute. He *(crash)* _____ into trees and *(find)* _____ safe and alive in the snow.

Using your grammar

1 Work in groups.

GROUP A: Look at page 130.
GROUP B: Look at the quiz on the right. Write full questions for numbers 4–6.

Answer all the questions. Then check your answers on page 127.

2 Ask the other group your questions. The group with the most correct answers wins.

1 When was Mount Everest first climbed? 1943, 1953 or 1963?
2 When is Hallowe'en celebrated? 31 September, 31 October or 31 November?
3 Where was the 1994 World Cup in soccer played? Italy, Spain or the USA?
4 Where / Martin Luther King / assassinated? Memphis, Dallas or New York?
5 Who / the play / *Hamlet* / written by? Homer, Shakespeare or Dickens?
6 In which country / champagne / produced? France, Germany or Italy?

VOCABULARY

News stories

1 Look at the extracts from newspapers on the right. Which is:

1 a headline? 3 an advertisement? 5 a horoscope?
2 a cartoon? 4 a weather forecast?

Killer shot dead in gunfight (c)

2 Look at the headline and article below. The word 'meet' has the sound /iː/ . What other spelling does /miːt/ have?

> ## No meet for us
>
> Marie Abbott (56) and Tony Lom (46), two butchers from Worthing, missed the most important appointment of their lives when

(d)

Cooler in most places with heavy clouds some sunshine. Winds are strong from the

CHALET HOLIDAYS

(e) BEAUTIFUL SWITZERLAND
Family-run chalet
Personal service
Excellent food and accommodation
Skiing, sauna, open fires
Telephone 01799 501504

3 Read the headlines below.

a) What other spelling could the underlined word(s) have?

I LOVE YOU <u>TWO</u>   DEN'S <u>WAIT</u> PROBLEM   <u>GOOD BUY</u>!
A <u>PEACE</u> OF PAPER   <u>WRITE</u> AND WRONG

b) Which headline is about:

1 children whose homework is bad?
2 a large person whose dinner didn't arrive on time?

4 Match the words in A and B to make expressions that often go together in news stories. Sometimes there is more than one possibility. Divide the expressions into two lists: 1 Good news; 2 Bad news.

A	B
car	record
bomb	champion
world	crash
tennis	block
road	explosion

Using your vocabulary

You are going to tell a news story about a traffic policeman.

a) Use a dictionary to find the meanings of the words in the box.

| throw away | baton | drivers | confused | lorry |

b) Work in groups.
GROUP A: Look at the picture on page 131.
GROUP B: Look at the picture on the right. What do you think is happening? What is going to happen? Now work with a partner from Group A. You start. Tell the story in your picture. Don't look at your partner's picture. Then listen while your partner tells his/her part of the story.

USE AND REVIEW

1 Read this newspaper article. Why were there more crimes in North Oxfordshire last year?

MY 1,800 THEFTS

A man who is a shoplifter and burglar has confessed to 1,800 crimes going back six years. The 25-year-old man lives in North Oxfordshire. He told his story after he got a two year prison sentence for burglary.

There were 24% more crimes in North Oxfordshire last year and 17% of them were his.

2 Look at the picture above. These are some of the things the police found. Talk about how much and how many things.
Examples:
They found a few traveller's cheques and a lot of cameras.

3 Sally and Kevin are talking about the criminal in the article above. Which are the correct words?

SALLY: I hear *someone / anyone / no one* was sent to prison for two years for burglary last week. *Anyone / No one* should go to prison for more than six months for a crime like that.

KEVIN: I don't agree. He confessed to 1,800 crimes. Have you heard of *someone / anyone / no one* who has committed so many crimes in North Oxfordshire?

SALLY: 1,800! That's *too much / too many* crimes for one person!

KEVIN: No, it's true. From some houses he didn't take *anything / nothing* important. Only silly things like bottles of Coke. *Everyone / Everything / Anyone* thinks he is crazy.

SALLY: That's terrible! I think he should go to prison for ten years. Two years is *very / too* short!

4 Work with a partner.

a) What do you think of the man's prison sentence?

b) What do you think of these punishments: 10 years in prison for murder, a £50 fine for dropping litter, 6 months in prison for stealing £5 and a £2,000 fine for robbing a bank? Use the words in the box.

too / very	long / short	little / much

Language reference

1 The passive

FORM

be (am / is / are) + past participle
The past participle of regular verbs is formed by adding *-ed* to the base form of the verb.
The past participles of common irregular verbs are on page 132.

Positive
She **is killed** at the end of the film. *French **is spoken** here.*
Negative
The window **isn't (is not) broken.** *This book **wasn't (was not) written** by a famous writer.* *Tea **isn't (is not) grown** in England. Cars **aren't (are not) made** in Madeira.*
Question
Is the window **broken?** *Why **isn't** tea **grown** in England?*

USE

We usually use the passive when we do not know, or are not interested in, who does something.
*Tea **is grown** in India.*
When we want to use the passive and say who or what did the action we use *by.*
*Jill was met **by** her brother.*

2 Active or passive?

In an active sentence we are usually more interested in **who** did the action.

Subject	Active verb	Object
Martin	*met*	*Jill.*

In a passive sentence we do not put the person who did the action at the beginning of the sentence.

Subject	Passive verb	
Jill	*was met*	**(by** *Martin).*

The object of an active sentence is the subject of a passive sentence.

Unit 17

•Celebration!•

USE YOUR ENGLISH

Special occasions

OCTOBER

Mon	Tue	Wed	Thu	Fri	Sat	Sun
		1	2	3	4	5
6	7	8	9	10	11	12
13	14	15	16	17	18	19
20	21	22	23	24	25	26
27	28	29	30	31		

NOVEMBER

Mon	Tue	Wed	Thu	Fri	Sat	Sun
					1	2
3	4	5	6	7	8	9
10	11	12	13	14	15	16
18	19	20	21	22	23	
25	26	27	28	29	30	

FEBRUARY

Mon	Tue	Wed	Thu	Fri	Sat	Sun
						1
6	7	8				
13	14	15				
20	21	22				
27	28					

JANUARY

			ed	Thu	Fri	Sat	Sun
				1	2	3	4
			7	8	9	10	11
			4	15	16	17	18
					23	24	25
				26			

DECEMBER

Mon	Tue	Wed	Thu	Fri	Sat	Sun
1	2	3	4	5	6	7
8	9	10	11	12	13	14
15	16	17	18	19	20	21
22	23	24	25	26	27	28
29	30	31				

1 The dates on the calendar are important in Britain. Do you know why? What happens on these days? Are any of them important in your country?

2 [▭ 17.1] Listen to these conversations.

a) Match the conversations with the dates on the calendar.
b) Find dates which match the pictures on the right.

3 What do we say on some important days? Match the words in A with those in B. For *Happy* there is more than one possibility.

A	B
Merry	New Year!
Happy	a good time!
Have	Christmas!
	birthday!

4 Work with a partner. Read these conversations.

1 A: I'm taking my driving test later today.
  B: Good luck!
2 A: It's my eighteenth birthday today.
  B: Congratulations!

a) In what other situations do we say 'Good luck!' and 'Congratulations!'?
b) Write short conversations for some of the situations.
c) Practise the conversations with your partner.

5 Work with a partner. Which dates do you think are important in your country? Tell him/her why.

SKILLS

Reading

1   Look at the pictures. What do you think Chinese New Year is like?

2   Read the article on the right about Chinese New Year and match the paragraphs with these questions. Example: 1 = C

1 How was the festival traditionally celebrated?
2 Why did the Chinese Government say there must be no more fireworks?
3 How long do the celebrations last?
4 How have the Chinese New Year celebrations changed?
5 What animal did 1994 have the name of?

3   Read the article again.

a) Make some notes about these questions.

  1 What do young people in China think? Example:
    They don't believe in superstitions.
  2 What happened when families went to other people's houses?
  3 What religious traditions are there at New Year?

b) Work with a partner. Compare your notes.

Vocabulary

1   What do these words mean? Choose a) or b). Can you guess from the article? Use a dictionary to help you, if necessary.

1 lanterns *n* (paragraph C)   a) bags   b) lights
2 lasted *v* (paragraph D)   a) continued   b) finished
3 banned *v* (paragraph E)   a) began   b) stopped

2   Find a word or expression that means:

1 shut *v* (paragraph A)   3 hurt *v* (paragraph E)
2 became adults *v*   4 not dangerous *adj*
  (paragraph D)   (paragraph E)

A   **T**he New Year's Festival in China can be in January or February. Although it is only a four-day holiday, China's offices often close down for nearly a month.

B   Every year has the name of one of the twelve animals of the Chinese zodiac, such as a cow, a rabbit or a monkey. 1994 was the year of the dog. People who are born in the year of the dog are believed to be quiet, faithful and friendly. If you were born in a dog year, then, as soon as the New Year begins, you should wear a red belt around your waist for good luck. However, young people in China do not believe in the superstition. 'I wore a belt when it was my year,' says 32-year-old driver Xiao Hung, 'and I had a lot of bad luck. I took it off.'

C   Mai-Tai remembers the New Year celebrations when she was a girl in the 1950s. In the evenings parents and children used to go on visits to the houses of their relatives and friends. They held lanterns to give them light in the dark streets. All around them, they could hear fireworks in the cold air. The door of each house had long pieces of red paper on it. Everywhere they went food was waiting for them, and they ate until they couldn't move. Relatives used to give the children money.

D   During the Cultural Revolution, which lasted from 1966 to 1976, religious traditions were stopped in China. But in the 1980s people once again began to kneel before the names of their ancestors at New Year. However, as many young people grew up during the Revolution, they aren't interested in the old traditions. They have started to celebrate some of the Western festivals like Christmas.

E   One part of the New Year which worried the Chinese Government was the tradition of fireworks, which got bigger and louder. In the countryside, fireworks were more like small bombs and hundreds of people were injured and killed. But in 1994 the Government banned fireworks to make the New Year safe for everyone.

Writing: paragraphs

1   Read this paragraph.
Put sentences 1–4 in the
correct order.

Christmas is the most important
public holiday in Britain.
1 On Christmas Day people give
   presents to each other and eat
   a large dinner.
2 Before Christmas, carols
   are sung and people send
   Christmas cards to their
   friends and relatives.
3 The day after Christmas Day is
   called Boxing Day and is also
   a public holiday.
4 Most people spend the
   holiday with their families.
Although Christmas was
originally a Christian festival,
many people today feel that it is
not religious any more.

2   Answer these questions
and make notes about a special
festival in your country.

1 How do people celebrate
   the festival?
2 What do people feel about
   the festival?

3   Write a paragraph using
your notes.
Begin your paragraph: *In my*
country ...
Middle sentences: Describe the
festival.
Last sentence: What do people
feel about the festival?

4   Ask yourself these
questions about your paragraph.

1 Is the paragraph clear and
   easy to understand?
2 Are the verb forms correct?
3 Are the linking expressions
   correct?
4 Are the spelling and
   punctuation correct?

GRAMMAR

Present Perfect Continuous: the unfinished past

1   Jon is a writer.

a) [▭ 17.2]   Read and listen to this conversation.
Then answer the questions.

ROSA: It's your birthday. You're not working, are you?
JON: I'm afraid so. I want to finish this novel.
ROSA: How long have you been writing it?
JON: Oh, for ages – since Christmas.

1 When did Jon start the novel?
2 Is he still writing it?

b) Look at the box and the pictures below. Complete the
sentences with the Present Perfect Continuous. Use the verb in
brackets.

I've *He's*	***been writing*** *a novel for three months.*

The Present Perfect Continuous is formed with *has/have been + -ing*
form of the verb.

1 Jon _____ on a novel since Christmas. *(work)*
2 She _____ computer games all morning. *(play)*
3 'I _____ Spanish since February.' *(learn)*

2 [17.3]   Jon and Rosa meet again in November. Read and listen to their conversation. Then answer the questions.

ROSA: Have you finished your novel yet?

JON: Yes. I finished it three weeks ago. I've written two short stories since then.

ROSA: Wow! What are you doing at the moment?

JON: I'm writing a play for television. I've been working on it for the last week.

ROSA: Amazing!

1 What has Jon written since he finished his novel?
2 Are the stories finished?
3 When did he start his play for television?
4 Is he still writing it?
5 Which verb forms are often used to talk about an action which started in the past and continues to the present? (See the *Language reference* on page 107 for verbs that do not usually take the *-ing* form.)

3   Read these sentences.

a) Which is the correct verb?

1 *Have you read / Have you been reading* that newspaper yet? Can I have it?
2 How long *have you been cleaning / have you cleaned* that car? *Haven't you finished / Haven't you been finishing* it yet?
3 How long *have you known / have you been knowing* Rosa?
4 He *is living / has been living* in Manchester since 1990.
5 She *has liked / has been liking* you since she saw you at that party.
6 I'm sorry I'm late. How long *are you waiting / have you been waiting?*
7 *I've played / I've been playing* tennis twice this week.
8 It *'s been raining / is raining* here all morning. It started at eight.

b) [17.4]   Listen and check your answers.

4 [17.5]   Listen to these conversations. How are these words pronounced: *has, have, been?*

1 A: How long has she been cleaning the car?
  B: For ages.
2 A: How long have you been living in Manchester?
  B: Since 1990.
3 A: Are you angry?
  B: Yes. I've been waiting for two hours.
4 A: How long has it been raining?
  B: All morning.

For and *since*

We use *since* to refer to a point in time (*1983, last week, our last holiday*) and *for* to refer to a period of time (*five years, four hours, a long time, ages*).

a) Do these expressions go with *for* or *since*?

six weeks	March
a year	yesterday
we met	my birthday
14 June	a few days
the end of the lesson	
6.45	three minutes

b) Make sentences with the Present Perfect Simple or Continuous and *for* or *since*. Example:
I / be a policeman / I left school
I've been a policeman since I left school.

1 he / watch television / three hours
2 she / not see him / a long time
3 he / talk on the phone / lunch time
4 they / play football / 3 o'clock
5 we / be married / 10 years

Using your grammar

On a piece of paper write ten things about yourself. Use the Present Simple or the Present Continuous. Write about:
• what you are wearing now.
• a habit.
• what your family and friends do.
• what you do in your free time.
• a place you often go to.

Work in groups. Mix up the papers. Take a piece of paper and guess who wrote it. Ask the person questions beginning *How long ...?* (Example: *How long have you had that jumper?*)

VOCABULARY

Having a party

1 Replace the underlined words with the correct form of the words from the box.

```
soft    celebrate    enjoy yourself
```

2 Which is the correct word?

1 A: Do you like parties?
  B: No, I find them *boring / bored / exciting*.
2 A: Hey, look at the band! Aren't they great?
  B: Yes, I always prefer *recorded / live* music.
3 A: Is John *drunk / sober*?
  B: Yes, I'm afraid he is. He can't stand up!

1 A: Are you <u>having a good time</u>?
  B: Yes, it's a great party.

2 A: What are we <u>having a party for</u>?
  B: Cindy's twenty-first birthday.

3 A: What about a glass of wine?
  B: Haven't you got any <u>non-alcoholic</u> drinks?

3 People often make mistakes with the words in italics.

a) Which is the correct word?

1 London has many *visitors / guests* every year.
2 My sister is a very good *cooker / cook*.
3 We study at a language school for *strangers / foreign students*.
4 We took a guided *tour / trip* round the museum.
5 Can you *learn / teach* me how to play the guitar?
6 I *lent / borrowed* you £50. Give it back.
7 Have you *passed / past* your exams?

b) Make sentences with three of the other words. Example:
We had fifty guests at our party last night.

Using your vocabulary

1 What makes a good party? Which of these ideas do you agree with? Add some ideas of your own.

- The best parties are always at the weekend and go on all night.
- There should be the same number of men and women.
- The music should be loud.
- There should be a lot of good food and drink.
- There should be a lot of games.
- The people should all know each other.
- There should be decorations.

2 Work in groups. You are going to have a party. Talk about the questions below. Then tell the class about your party.

1 What is the party for? (your sister's birthday? your class?)
2 Where? (at the school? at a restaurant?)
3 When? (in the middle of the day?)
4 Who should come? (a few friends? other students? everyone?)
5 What kind of food do you want?
6 What kind of music do you want?

USE AND REVIEW

1 Work with a partner.

a) STUDENT A
Look at page 131.

STUDENT B
What are the past participles of these verbs:
hear, sell, wear, break, understand, put, think,
say, speak?

b) Ask your partner about the past participles
of your verbs. Write down his/her answers.
Don't say if the answer is correct or not.
Example:
B: *What is the past participle of hear?*
A: *Heard.*

c) Your partner is going to ask you about some
past participles.

d) Check your answers on page 132. Who got
the most correct answers?

2 These are some pieces of 'good news'.
Write the 'bad news'. Use the words in brackets
to help you. Use the passive. Example:
The art gallery bought the painting for $1 million.
(steal / last night)
The painting was stolen last night.

1 The singer is giving a concert in Rome.
(tickets / sell out)
2 I saw an expensive glass bowl in the shop.
(break / child)
3 There was a bottle of wine in the cupboard.
(drink / last week)
4 John looked well yesterday morning.
(take to hospital / yesterday evening)
5 The President was very popular. *(assassinate
in 1994 / someone from another country)*

3 Make sentences from these headlines. Are
they good or bad news?

(a) Airport closed by bad weather
(b) More CDs sold last year
(c) FILM STAR'S NEW BABY
(d) Ice-skater breaks leg
(e) MISSING SCULPTURE FOUND
(f) Train crash in Sweden

Language reference

1 Present Perfect Continuous

FORM

Have/has + been + base form of verb + -ing

Positive
I**'ve been playing** all day.
Negative
She **hasn't been playing** all day.
Question
How long **have** they **been playing?**
Have you **been playing** for a long time?

USE

We use the Present Perfect Continuous to talk about things
that started in the past and are still going on now.
> I**'ve been living** here since 1992. (I started living here
> in 1992 and I am still living here.)

```
              ╭  x I've been living here            ╮
  ←──────────────────────────────────────────────→│
  PAST        since      for a long            NOW
              1992       time
```

Note that we do NOT say: ~~I'm living here since 1992~~.

2 *For* or *since*?

For (**for** a long time) and since (**since** 1992) say how long
something has been happening.
> How long have you been learning French?
> I've been learning French | **for** six months.
> | **since** 1994.

For is used with a period of time. (**for** two years, six
months, a long time)
Since is used with a point in time. (**since** 1992, July, 10.30,
4th June)

3 Present Perfect Simple or Present Perfect Continuous?

We can also use the Present Perfect Simple to talk about
events that started in the past and are still going on now.
> I**'ve lived** here since 1992.

There is often little difference between the Present Perfect
Continuous and the Present Perfect Simple. However we
usually use the Present Perfect Continuous when we are
thinking of the action.
> I**'ve been working** here since 1982.

Verbs that express a state, not an action, do **not** usually
take an *-ing* form:
like, know, love, be, have.
> I**'ve liked** you since I saw you at the disco.

Note that we do NOT say: ~~I've been liking you...~~

•Love your neighbour•

USE YOUR ENGLISH

Being polite

1   Look at the pictures.

a) What do you think the people are saying?
b) [▭ 18.1]   Listen to these conversations. Match the conversations with the pictures.
c) Complete these sentences.

    1 Oh, _____ give me a hand with these, please?
    2 Oh, _____ get me some stamps, please?
    3 _____ but have you got any change?
    4 Tom. Excuse me, _____ give me a push?
    5 _____ looking after Oscar for a few days?

d) Which expression/s do we use when:

    1 we don't know the other person very well?
    2 we think the request is difficult for the other person?

e) Someone asks you to do something. What do you say when:

    1 you agree to the request?
    2 you don't agree to the request?

2   Work in groups. Ask each other to do things politely. Use the nouns and verbs in the boxes or use your own words. If you do not agree to the request, you must give a good reason.

NOUNS	VERBS
window pencil board £5 door seat time	lend open/close draw pick up take clean tell move write

3   Work with a partner. Write conversations for some of these situations.

1 You want a taxi driver to drive you from London to Edinburgh.
2 You ordered a salad but the waiter has brought you a steak.
3 You are locked out of your flat. You want a neighbour to help you get in.
4 You are in front of the White House in Washington and you want a stranger to take a photograph of you.
5 It's three o'clock in the morning. You have a plane to catch at seven and must get some sleep. Ask your friend to wake you at five.

SKILLS

Listening and speaking

1   What are the advantages and disadvantages of living in this kind of house? The two men are neighbours. They are having an argument. What do you think the problem is?

a) What do you think? Complete these sentences.

1 Having neighbours is good because _____.
2 Having neighbours is bad because _____.
3 I'd love to have neighbours who _____.
4 I'd hate to have neighbours who _____.

b) Work with a partner. Compare your answers and tell each other about your neighbours.

2   Work in two groups.

GROUP A
[📼 18.2]   Listen to Henry Skitt talking about his neighbour, Tim Dodd, and his friends. Answer these questions.

1 What does Henry think of his neighbours' music?
2 What did the police do about it?
3 Why hasn't Henry been to work?
4 What do the young people do in Henry's garden?
5 If Tim told Henry he was going to have a party, what would Henry do?

GROUP B
[📼 18.3]   Listen to Tim Dodd talking about Mr Skitt. Answer these questions.

1 What didn't Tim know about Henry?
2 When does Tim play loud music? Why?
3 When was the last time Tim had a party?
4 What noise does Tim hear from his neighbour?
5 Why does Tim play his drums in the cellar?

3   Work with a partner from the other group. Ask for the answers to their questions.

4   Talk to your partner about these questions.

1 Is Henry Skitt right to complain? Give your reasons.
2 What advice would you give Henry and Tim?
3 Should it be against the law to make too much noise? Give your reasons.
4 In your country, can you ask the police to come if your neighbours make too much noise?
5 Which of these can/can't you do where you live?

   • have a pet
   • hang washing outside
   • have an untidy garden
   • leave rubbish outside
   • beep your car horn at night

6 Are there any other rules where you live?

Vocabulary: phrasal verbs

Here are some phrasal verbs which Henry and Tim used.

- *I have to **lie down**.*
- *I've **been off** work.*
- *They can always **come round**.*
- *We're not going to **get into** a fight.*
- *I play music to **wake** myself **up**.*

Use them to complete the sentences.

1 Will you _____ _____ to my house and see me later?
2 I feel tired. I'm going to _____ _____ on the bed for a few minutes. Can you _____ me _____ at six?
3 I don't want to _____ _____ an argument about who's right and who's wrong.
4 Julia isn't well. She is going to _____ _____ school tomorrow.

Writing: phrasal verbs

Phrasal verbs are usually informal. Rewrite these notes. Replace the underlined words with one of the phrasal verbs in brackets. Use the correct form of the verb.

① *Take the motorway and <u>leave</u> at the first exit. Ring the bell when you <u>arrive</u> at the house.*
(turn up, turn off)

② *I'm going to <u>stop coming</u> here if you don't repair the lift. It <u>stopped working</u> again this morning.*
(give up, break down)

③ *Sorry I was late home last night, darling. I had to <u>go somewhere with</u> an important customer. I hope you didn't <u>keep awake</u> waiting for me.*
(stay up, take out)

GRAMMAR

Sentence patterns (1): verb + person

1 Read this extract from a famous children's story.

'I'm going shopping in the village,' George's mother said to George on Saturday morning. 'So be a good boy ... And don't forget to give Grandma her medicine at eleven o'clock.' Then out she went, closing the back door behind her.

	SUBJECT	VERB	OBJECT/ PERSON	TO + BASE FORM OF VERB
'Be a good boy,' George's mother said.	She	**told**	George	to be a good boy.
'Don't forget to give Grandma her medicine,' George's mother said.	She	**asked**	him	**not** to forget to give Grandma her medicine.

2 Read the next part of the story and complete the sentences.

'Now you heard what your mother said, George. Don't forget my medicine.'
'No, Grandma,' George said.
'And try to behave well while she is away.'
'Yes, Grandma,' George said.

1 Grandma _____ George not to _____.
2 Grandma _____ George to _____ well.

3   Read the next part of the story.

'**Y**ou can make me a nice cup of tea for a start,'
Grandma said to George.
'Yes, Grandma,' George said.
George really disliked Grandma.
'How much sugar in your tea today, Grandma?' he asked her.
'One spoon,' she said. 'And no milk ...'
George went into the kitchen and made Grandma a cup of tea
with a teabag. He put one spoon of sugar in it and no milk.
He stirred the tea well and carried the cup into the living room.
Grandma sipped the tea. 'It's not sweet enough,' she said.
'Put more sugar in.'

(from *George's Marvellous Medicine* by Roald Dahl)

Make sentences with the words below. Example:
She / make / nice cup of tea.
She told/asked George to make her a nice cup of tea.

1 She / put in / one spoon
   of sugar.

2 She / not / put any milk in.
3 She / put more sugar in.

Sentence patterns (2): reported sentences

Say or *tell?*

'I'm only a little boy, Grandma,' George said.		
	OBJECT / PERSON	
George **said**		*(that) he **was** only a little boy.*
George **told**	Grandma / her	

a) Complete these sentences with *said* or *told*.

1 Sarah _____ me it was her birthday.
2 He _____ he didn't like tennis.
3 She _____ Mike they never went out.
4 Nikki _____ she knew the way.
5 Carlos _____ her not to shout.

b) Write reported sentences with *say* or *tell*. Example:
  'I'm going out.'   *John said he was going out.*

1 'We want to see the film.'   Sally and Peter _____.
2 'I'm watching television later.' Tony _____.
3 'We like Disneyland.'   Emma _____ her _____.
4 'I'm very happy.'   Mary _____.
5 'Greg is hungry.'   Tina _____ Sonia that _____.

Using your grammar

Work in groups of three.

STUDENT A
Look at page 131.

STUDENT A
Look at page 131.

> STUDENT B
> You are from the same family
> as Student A. Choose how
> you are related. Are you
> husband and wife, brother
> and sister, parent and child?
> You have had an argument.
> You are angry with Student A
> because he/she:
> • gives orders
> • gets up early and makes
>   a noise.
> • never wants to go out.
>
> Make a list of other things
> you are angry about (money,
> parties, TV, clothes, car etc).
> Your aren't speaking to
> Student A but Student C is a
> go-between. Ask him/her to
> help you.

> STUDENT C
> Student A and Student B
> aren't speaking to each other.
> You are a go-between. Help
> Students A and B with their
> lists. Begin with Student B.
> Tell Student B about Student
> A and Student A about
> Student B. Examples:
> *He says you are lazy. She
> told me you never help in
> the house. She asked me to
> tell you ...*
> Try to get Students A and B
> to be friends again.

VOCABULARY

Doing things in the house

Look at the pictures on the right.

a) Match them with the verbs in the box.

iron	decorate	dust	hoover	wash up	tidy up

b) Make sentences about the pictures using the words in the box.
Example:
He's doing the ironing.

c) What other jobs are there to do in the house?

Do or *make*?

> DO – work, general action
> They **did** the ironing.   He **did** the housework.   She **did** her homework.
>
> MAKE – create something, a particular action
> He **made** a pizza.   He **made** a mistake.   They **made** a noise.
>
> Note: **make** the bed = tidy the sheets and blankets

Complete these sentences with the correct form of *do* or *make*.
Use a dictionary to help you.

1 A: Hurry up. You must _____ the cleaning.
  B: No, I hate _____ housework.
2 A: Sorry, dear. I've _____ a mistake. I _____ you a cup
    of tea but I put salt in it instead of sugar!
  B: You idiot! And you've _____ a mess in the kitchen.
    Can't you _____ anything right?
  A: Shall I go and _____ the washing?
  B: No. I'll _____ that. You go and _____ the bed.
3 A: Why do your children always _____ such a noise?
    Why don't you keep them quiet?
  B: Sorry, but I _____ my best.

Using your vocabulary

Look at the pictures on the right.

a) In your country which jobs do men do? Which jobs do women
do? Which jobs do *you* do? Make three lists.

b) Who does the jobs which you don't do?

c) Work with a partner. Compare your lists.

USE AND REVIEW

1   Talk to other students in the class.
Find someone who:

1 can tell you the difference between a *stranger*
and a *foreigner*.
2 knows another word for a *non-alcoholic* drink.
3 can explain the difference between a *cooker*
and a *cook*.
4 knows what *live* music is.
5 can give you one sentence with *lend* and
one sentence with *borrow*.

2   Work in two groups.

GROUP A: You are John Smith. You want a job as
the editor of a newspaper in the USA.
GROUP B: You are Sophie Evans. You want a job
as an airline pilot in Australia.

a) Fill in this application form for your person.

APPLICATION FORM FOR THE JOB OF

_____

NAME _____

AGE   DATE OF BIRTH

EXPERIENCE   I have worked ...

            I have lived ...

            I have been studying ...

PRESENT OCCUPATION   I am working ...

INTERESTS   I like ...

---

b) Work with a partner from the other group.
Read your partner's application form and then
interview him/her for the job. Ask questions
with *what / when / how long have you...?*

Language reference

1 Subject + verb + person + *to* + base form of the verb

Subject	Verb	Object person	To + Base form
'Go!'			
I/ You/ We/ They He/ She/ It	asked told	her/ him/ it	to go.
'Don't go!'			
I/ You/ We/ They He/ She/ It	asked told	us/me/you/them	**not** to go.

2 *Say* or *tell?*

We *say* **something**.
   He says (that) ***it is late***.
We *tell* **a person** something.
   He told ***us*** *(that) he was not very well.*

3 Reported sentences

We use this form when we report what a person said.
Exact words:
   'I'm going out.'
Reported words:
   He says (that) he is going out.
   He said (that) he was going out.
   He said to me (that) he was going out.
   He tells me (that) he's going out.
   He told me (that) he was going out.
When we use *said* or *told* (past tense) the reported
statement (*'I'm going out'*) is often in the past.
   He ***said****/****told*** *me he* ***was going*** *out.*
It is not necessary to use *that*.

•Team spirit•

USE YOUR ENGLISH

Talking about different cultures

1   Look at the pictures. Ayu has just arrived in Britain from Indonesia.

a) What is Zoë saying? Can you guess? She is telling Ayu what to do:

> A to order drinks in a pub.
> B if she is invited to someone's house for dinner.
> C to attract the waiter's attention in a restaurant.
> D when she greets someone for the first time.
> E if she stays with a family.

b) [🖭 19.1]   Listen to extracts from Zoë and Ayu's conversation. Match each extract with one of the pictures.

c) Listen again. What advice does Zoë give? Example:
Always order at the bar.

d) What are the differences between Britain and your country?

2   In your country are there any laws about:

- dropping litter?
- riding bicycles?
- when shops can and can't open?
- crossing the road?

3   In your country are there any rules or customs about:

- giving your seat to old people on a bus?
- how people should dress? (for example, at work)
- tipping? (for example, in a taxi)
- people touching each other? (for example, in the street)
- greeting each other?
- what you do when you watch a sport? (for example, do you clap? do you boo? do you shout?)
- giving and receiving presents?

4   Work with a partner. A British tourist is coming to your country. Make a list of DOs and DON'Ts like the example on the right.

DO	DON'T
Drive on the right	Touch people on the head

SKILLS

Reading

1   Look at the picture and answer these questions.

1 How many *teams* are there?
2 What is the *stadium*?
3 Who is the *referee*?
4 Where are the *supporters*?
5 Which player has *scored* a *goal*?
6 Manchester United are playing in Manchester. Is it a *home match* or an *away match*?
7 At the end of the match the score was Manchester United 3, Chelsea 1. Who *won*?
8 Did Chelsea *beat* Manchester?

2   Read the article. Which paragraphs tell us the answers to these questions? Example: 1=*B*

1 How did Sister Paola first become interested in football?
2 How did she first become a TV star?
3 What do the Lazio players think of her?
4 What was the result of the Lazio-Milan game?

3   Answer these questions.

1 What is the 'big day'? (paragraph A)
2 Why is the referee a 'cheat'? (paragraph A)
3 When does Sister Paola punch the air?
4 How long has she liked football?
5 What does she do with the Lazio players?

4   These are some answers. What are the questions? Example: Lazio.
Which team does Sister Paola support?

1 Twenty years ago.
2 No, AC Milan beat Lazio.
3 She goes back to her teaching.

Team spirit

A The crowds are in Rome's Olympic Stadium for the big day. Their team, Lazio, are playing AC Milan. Millions of people are sitting in front of their TV sets. 'The referee is a cheat,' cries a well-known voice. 'That's why he didn't allow our team's great goal – but then, he comes from Milan!' This is Sister Paola, a 46-year-old nun. She is mad about Lazio. When they score, she punches the air. When they miss an easy goal, she covers her face.

B She became a Lazio supporter twenty years ago when some children asked her to teach them about the game. She says: 'I thought I'd better go and watch Lazio. Then I became very keen on football.' So every Sunday when Lazio play at home – after attending Mass – Sister Paola walks down from the convent to the stadium, talking to the fans.

C Then, recently, she learnt that the father of one of her pupils was a television sports reporter. She asked to go into the studio to see Lazio's away games. There a TV director thought he saw a possible star. The only question was, what would a nun, without make-up, and wearing simple clothes, be like on camera, with a microphone in her hand?

D She was very good. People love to listen to her with her passion and love of football. And she is just as popular with the Lazio players. 'I talk about their problems and say prayers with them,' she says.

E But today against the champions her prayers are not enough. AC Milan have beaten Lazio 1-0. The colour in her pale face disappears and her voice gets quieter. 'I don't know what to say,' she tells her fans. 'This is a terrible moment for us all.'

F Then she returns to her work of the week, her prayers and her teaching, her prison visiting and her work with the poor.

(from *The Mail on Sunday*)

Vocabulary

Find a word or phrase in the article about Sister Paola that means:

1 large numbers of people (paragraph A)
2 hits with the hand closed (paragraph A)
3 puts her hands in front of it (paragraph A)
4 strong feelings (paragraph D)
5 almost white (paragraph E)

Writing

1 Read this sentence and answer the questions.
'The referee is a cheat,' cries a well-known voice.

1 What are Sister Paola's words?
2 Which punctuation marks show her words?
3 Where is the comma?

2 Punctuate these sentences:

1 Im going out she said
2 What are you thinking he asked her
3 I wont do it I told him

3 Rewrite this story. Use speech marks and commas where necessary.

She told me about her husband. He's a Chelsea supporter. Really? I said. How could you live with him? She saw the look on my face. Why don't you tell him to support Manchester United or you'll divorce him? She laughed. You're crazy, you know. Really crazy she said.

GRAMMAR

Verb patterns (1): the future

If, when, as soon as, unless

1 Tim is 14. His Swiss uncle has invited him to go on holiday in Switzerland. He has booked a hotel room for Tim. Tim is saying goodbye to his parents.

a) [💿 19.2] Listen and complete the sentences.

1 What are you going to do when you _____ there?
2 I'll call you as soon as I _____.
3 What will you do if he _____ not there when you _____?
4 He won't come and pick you up unless you _____.

b) What verb form do we use after *if, when, as soon as* and *unless* to talk about the future?

c) Read these sentences.
When you see him, give him our love.
If you see him, give him our love.

1 In which sentence will Tim definitely see his uncle?
2 In which sentence is it possible he won't see him?

d) Which is the correct word?

1 *When / If* it's fine tomorrow, we'll go for a swim. I hope it is.
2 *When / If* you get back from your trip, I'll cook you a nice meal. See you next week.

e) *Unless* usually means 'if not'. Complete these sentences with *if* or *unless*. Examples:
Unless you hurry, you'll miss the plane.
If you don't hurry, you'll miss the plane.

1 _____ he phones, tell him I'm out.
2 _____ you are careful, you'll have an accident.

2 *As soon as* is like *when*. It means *at the moment that*. Complete these sentences. Use the correct form of the word in brackets. Example:
As soon as I see him, I *(tell)* _____ him.
As soon as I see him, I'll tell him.

1 Don't forget to clean your teeth when you *(get up)* _____.
2 You won't pass your exams unless you *(study)* _____.
3 If you know the answer, please *(not tell)* _____ me.
4 I'll buy some coffee as soon as the shop *(open)* _____.
5 Unless we hurry, we *(be)* _____ late.
6 When I see her, I *(invite)* _____ her.
7 There are a lot of trains. Don't worry if you *(miss)* _____ it.
8 As soon as it stops snowing, we *(go)* _____ out.

Verb patterns (2)

Verb + 2 objects

Tim's mother says, '*Give it to him as soon as you see him.*'

When *give* has two objects we can make the sentence in two ways.

Give	THING/OBJECT *the **present*** (noun) *it* (pronoun)	→	PERSON/OBJECT *to your **uncle*** (noun). *to **him*** (pronoun).
Give	PERSON/OBJECT *your **uncle*** (noun) ***him*** (pronoun)	←	THING/OBJECT *the **present*** (noun).

We don't usually say *Give your uncle **it*** or *Give him **it***.

1   John is talking to Simon. Read these sentences and answer the questions.

a) *Give the camera to your brother.*

b) *Give it to your brother.*

c) *Give your brother the camera.*

1 What does John tell Simon to give?
2 Who must Simon give it to?
3 In each sentence above underline the answer to 1.
4 In each sentence circle the answer to 2.
5 What preposition comes after the thing and before the person?

2   Look at the *Language reference* on page 119.

a) Which other verbs follow the same patterns as *give?*

b) Write sentences with these words. Put them in the correct order. Add any other necessary words. Begin: *Please ...*

1 him / the message / give
2 later / it / give / her
3 the book / him / take
4 the children / read / a story
5 the way / me / show
6 the money / me / lend

3   What do you think the people below are saying?

Using your grammar

Work with a partner. Write some instructions for a secret agent's next job.

a) Think about the answers to these questions.

- What is the mission? (to steal a bomb? to stop someone killing the president?)
- Who is the agent going to meet? (another agent? the president's wife?)

b) Write instructions using *when, if, as soon as, unless.* Examples:
When you get there, go to the ... (hotel, palace)
If you see him, give him the ... (message, photos)
Unless you ... (say the password, carry a gun)

a

pass

b

bring

c

send

d

show

VOCABULARY

Sports

1 Look at the pictures and say what the sport is.

a) Find a word from the box for each picture.

| costume | ring | club | pool | course | pitch |
| gloves | track | shorts | court | ball | racket |

b) What other words from the box go with each picture?
Example: 1 = *court*

2 Do we use *go* or *play* with these sports? Use a dictionary to help you.

jogging   basketball   skiing   baseball
windsurfing   squash   ice-skating   football

3 What is happening in the pictures on the right?

a) Match the pictures with these sentences.

   1 The horse *kicked* me.
   2 Jane *hit* him on the head with a book.
   3 He *ran* to catch the bus.
   4 She *threw* her coat on the floor.
   5 Tom *bounced* the baby on his knee.
   6 He *punched* the man on the nose.

b) Find a sport in Exercises 1 and 2 above for each of the verbs
in italics in Exercise 3a). Example: kick = *football*

Using your vocabulary

1 What exercise do you take? How often do you do it? Examples:
*I walk home every evening. I do exercises every morning. I go
swimming once a week. I do the housework on Saturdays.*

2 Find the student in the class who is most similar to you.

USE AND REVIEW

1   Write down five true and five false sentences about yourself. Examples:
I live on a boat. My father works in a bank.

a) Work with a partner. Choose someone you don't know very well. Guess if your partner's sentences are true.

b) Report back to the class. Example:
Thomas told me he lived on a boat but it's not true.

2   Look at this picture above for one minute and close your books.

a) What can you remember? Write down as many sentences as you can. Example:
A woman is making the bed upstairs.

b) Work with a partner. Compare your sentences.

Language reference

1 Verb patterns (1): the future with *if, when, as soon as, unless*

When we use the conjunctions *if, when, as soon as* and *unless* to talk about the future, we use a present verb form (often the Present Simple).

FORM

	Present	
If **When** **As soon as**	*it's*	*sunny, I'll go out.*
Unless	*it's*	*sunny, I won't go out.*

USE

a) *when*
   When means it's sure to happen.
   *I'm going to Oxford. **When** I'm there, I'll see my brother.*

b) *if*
   If means it will possibly happen.
   *Perhaps I'll go to Oxford. **If** I go, I'll see my brother.*

c) *unless*
   Unless means *if not*.
   *I can't hear you **unless** you shout.*
   (*I can't hear you **if** you do**n't** shout.*)

d) *as soon as*
   As soon as means *when /at the moment that.*
   *I'll leave **as soon as** I can.*

2 Verb patterns (2): Verb + 2 objects

Some verbs have two objects.

a) Pattern 1

	Verb	Person (Indirect object)	Thing (Direct object)
I	*gave*	*my friend* *him*	*a car.*

b) Pattern 2

	Verb	Thing (Direct object)	Person (to + Indirect object)
I	*gave*	*a car* *it*	*to my friend.* *to him.*

Other verbs which follow the same patterns: *read, show, pass, bring, send, lend, pay, sell, take.*
Note that we cannot say: ~~I gave my friend it.~~

•Going away•

USE YOUR ENGLISH

Booking in

1 Anna booked into a hotel this afternoon.

a) What did she do? Put the pictures in the correct order and then make sentences.

b) Can you complete her conversation with the receptionist?

unpack / suitcase

RECEPTIONIST: Good afternoon. Can I _____ ?
ANNA: Yes, I've _____ a room for two nights.
RECEPTIONIST: _____ ?
ANNA: Anna Escobar.
RECEPTIONIST: Single or _____ ?
ANNA: Single.
RECEPTIONIST: Do you want a room with a _____ or a shower ?
ANNA: A shower, please.
RECEPTIONIST: Just _____ this form, please.
ANNA: Certainly. How much _____ a night?
RECEPTIONIST: £68 with breakfast. How _____ ?
ANNA: With American Express. Is that OK?
RECEPTIONIST: Fine. How much _____ ?
ANNA: Just these two suitcases.
RECEPTIONIST: _____ is 220. Breakfast _____ 7.00 to 9.30. _____ an evening meal?
ANNA: No, thanks. _____ a traveller's cheque later?
RECEPTIONIST: Of course, here's your key. Enjoy your stay.

c) [📼 20.1] Listen and check your answers.

2 Work with a partner.

> **STUDENT A**
> Look at page 131.

> **STUDENT B**
> You are the receptionist at the Swan Hotel. Use the information on the right to answer Student A's questions.

hotel bus / from airport

porter / tip

check in / reception

Swan Hotel

Large house 2 miles from city centre in quiet residential area.
Friendly family atmosphere.
Some bedrooms with private bathroom or shower.
En-suite toilets in many rooms.
Central heating six months of the year.
Comfortable restaurant overlooking the garden.
Small cocktail bar.
Street parking nearby.
TV room.
No pets or children.
Price per person per night: £75.

SKILLS

Reading and speaking

1 These people had bad holiday experiences. What do you think happened to them?

2 Work in three groups.

GROUP A

a) Read Maureen's postcard. Which picture does it describe?

b) Complete these sentences.

1 On Maureen's earlier holiday in Florida there were _____.
2 When she went to Australia _____.
3 She thought this holiday was going to be different because she was _____.
4 Unfortunately, at the airport she took _____.

GROUP B

a) Read Leslie's postcard. Which picture does it describe?

b) Complete these sentences.

1 Leslie wanted to catch _____.
2 He took his wife and children to the _____.
3 When he tried to drive the car onto the train, the guards _____.
4 Unfortunately, the train that he and his family were on was going _____.

GROUP C

a) Read Claire's postcard. Which picture does it describe?

b) Complete these sentences.

1 Claire wanted her holiday in the Caribbean to be _____.
2 There were problems with _____.
3 The tour they took was also bad because the taxi driver _____.
4 Unfortunately, she had to stay for two weeks although she _____.

3 Find a partner from each of the other groups and tell them 'your' story.

4 What bad holiday experiences have *you* had?

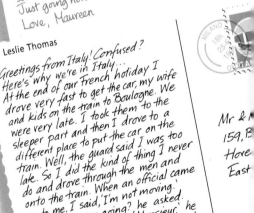

1 Maureen Lipman

Well, after the typhoons in Florida, the worst weather for 60 years in Tenerife, and two weeks of non-stop rain in Australia, I thought this was going to be different. I was the first person to get my bags at the airport - which usually never happens to me - and the hotel was excellent. Then the phone rang. 'Ms Lipman?' said a voice. 'Yes?' I said. 'I think I've got your suitcase,' said a voice.
Just going now to change the suitcase.
Love, Maureen

2 Leslie Thomas

Greetings from Italy! Confused?
Here's why we're in Italy...
At the end of our French holiday I drove very fast to get the car, my wife and kids on the train to Boulogne. We were very late. I took them to the sleeper part and then I drove to a different place to put the car on the train. Well, the guard said I was too late. So I did the kind of thing I never do and drove through the men and onto the train. When an official came up to me, I said, 'I'm not moving.' 'Where are you going?' he asked. 'Boulogne,' I replied. 'Monsieur,' he said, 'this train is going to Milan.'
See you soon! Leslie

3 Claire Rayner

When we came to the Caribbean we were looking forward to a very comfortable holiday. But, it's awful. The hotel's terrible - the plughole in our washbasin isn't connected to the pipe and there's water all over the bedroom floor. I went for a swim in the pool and came face to face with a rat! We decided to take a tour. But the taxi driver wouldn't go faster than 5mph. Worst of all, we've booked for two weeks and can't get an early flight home, so we'll have to stay.
See you on the 10th, Claire

(from *Good Housekeeping*)

Listening

1   Read this extract from a questionnaire about holidays.
What do you like/dislike? Put the things in each list in the correct
order for you under A (1 = the things I like/dislike most).

LIKE	A You	B British people said	C %	DISLIKE	A You	B British people said	C %
1 Visiting museums and art galleries	—	—	—	1 Noisy and rude people	—	—	—
2 Spending more time with family and friends	—	—	—	2 Packing to go on holiday	—	—	—
3 Drinking a lot	—	—	—	3 Fighting to get a place by the pool	—	—	—
4 Seeing life in different countries	—	—	—	4 No information about delays	—	—	—
5 Enjoying the beauties of nature	—	—	—	5 Waiting at the airport	—	—	—
6 New kinds of food	—	—	—	6 Not speaking the language	—	—	—
7 Meeting new people	—	—	—	7 Traffic jams	—	—	—
8 Lying on the beach	—	—	—	8 Getting lost and arguing with each other	—	—	—
9 Just being away from home and the daily routine	—	—	—	9 Paying too much for things	—	—	—

2   What do British people like and dislike about holidays?

a) What do *you* think? Choose one thing from each list.

b) [🔊 20.2]   Listen to the results of a survey on holidays and the British. Were your guesses correct?

c) Listen again. Put the things in each list in the correct order for the British under B (1 = the things they like/dislike most).

d) Listen again and complete the percentages (%) under C.

Writing: linking words

Read about Posy Simmonds' experience and complete the
sentences. Use each word from the box once.

| finally and but so when then because after |

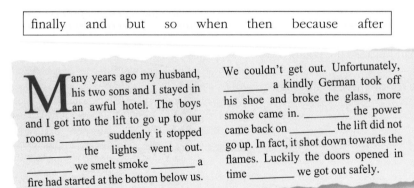

Many years ago my husband, his two sons and I stayed in an awful hotel. The boys and I got into the lift to go up to our rooms _____ suddenly it stopped _____ the lights went out. _____ we smelt smoke _____ a fire had started at the bottom below us.

We couldn't get out. Unfortunately, _____ a kindly German took off his shoe and broke the glass, more smoke came in. _____ the power came back on _____ the lift did not go up. In fact, it shot down towards the flames. Luckily the doors opened in time _____ we got out safely.

Grammar

1 Mixed practice

Bill and Pat are at an exhibition of paintings and sculpture by the artist Pablo Picasso.

a) Which is the correct expression?

PAT: How long *are you / have you been* a fan of Picasso?

BILL: A long time. But I *haven't seen / didn't see* any of his paintings *for / since* the Paris exhibition in 1966. In those days I *used to find / find* it difficult to understand his work.

PAT: I *used to go / went* to an exhibition of his in New York, in 1973, the year he died. I *am / have been* waiting for an exhibition like this to come to London *for / since* years.

BILL: Me too.

PAT: Look at this sculpture of Jacqueline. It says in the programme that it *made / was made* by Picasso's assistants from a paper model.

BILL: Yes, it's *very / too* interesting. I like things *who / which* are a bit different.

PAT: I *said / told* Louise to come when she *has / will have* the time. I want *her to see / that she sees* some of these paintings.

BILL: Yes, Louise is *someone / anyone* who would like Picasso.

b) [20.3]   Listen and check your answers.

2 The Second Conditional

Join the sentences using a Second Conditional. Example:
I don't live in London. I don't go to the Tate Gallery.
If I lived in London, I would go to the Tate Gallery.

1 I don't know her address. I can't write to her.
2 She doesn't work. She hasn't any money.
3 I don't go swimming. I'm not fit.
4 I won't invite you to the theatre. I haven't got another ticket.
5 It is snowing. We can't go out.

3 Making comparisons

Complete the table.

ADJECTIVE	COMPARATIVE	SUPERLATIVE
good	better	_____
bad	_____	the worst
hardworking	_____	_____
happy	happier	_____
comfortable	_____	the most comfortable
big	_____	_____

4 Question tags

a) What is the question tag in each sentence?

1 There's something wrong, _____ ?
2 He likes jazz, _____ ?
3 She didn't try, _____ ?
4 It wasn't very nice, _____ ?
5 Tom's very attractive, _____ ?

b) [20.4]   Listen and check your answers.

Pronunciation

Weak forms and contractions

a) [20.5]   Listen to these sentences. How many words are there in each sentence? A contracted form *(he's)* is two words.

1 _____ you.
2 If _____ address _____.
3 I _____ rich.
4 He _____ watch _____ birthday.
5 How long _____ London?
6 Give _____ him _____.

b) Listen again and complete the sentences.

Vocabulary

1 Phrasal verbs

a) Replace the expressions in italics with a phrasal verb from the box. Put the phrasal verbs in the correct form. Example:
Phil *was Sue's boyfriend* for two years.
*Phil **went out with** Sue for two years.*

hang on	go out with	take off	break down
sell out	stay up	grow up	fill in
split up	look after		

1 Please *complete* this application form.
2 *Their relationship finished* last week. (They ...)
3 *Wait* a minute! Don't go.
4 I wanted to go to the football match but *there were no more tickets*. (The tickets were ...)
5 *Take care of* the children while I'm away.
6 If you are hot, *remove* your coat.
7 What do you want to do when you *are an adult* ?
8 My car *is not working*. (It has ...)
9 I *didn't go to bed* until midnight.

b) Complete the sentences with the correct form of one of the verbs in Exercise 1a).

1 When I arrived at the airport I had to *fill in an immigration form.*
2 We weren't tired so we decided to _____.
3 I was travelling to work when the train _____.
4 The class finishes in five minutes. Can you _____ ?
5 My brother's not very well. Can you _____ him?
6 You're like a child. Why don't you _____ ?

2 Correct or incorrect?

Are these sentences correct or incorrect? Tick or cross the first box. Then bet between 10 and 50 points on each: 50 points = you're sure you are right; 10 points = you're not sure you're right. If you are right, you win the number of points you bet. If you are wrong, you lose the number of points you bet.

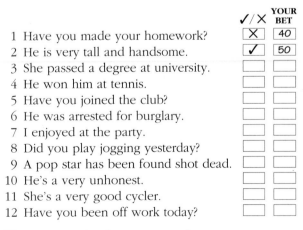

		✓ / ✗	YOUR BET
1	Have you made your homework?	✗	40
2	He is very tall and handsome.	✓	50
3	She passed a degree at university.		
4	He won him at tennis.		
5	Have you joined the club?		
6	He was arrested for burglary.		
7	I enjoyed at the party.		
8	Did you play jogging yesterday?		
9	A pop star has been found shot dead.		
10	He's a very unhonest.		
11	She's a very good cycler.		
12	Have you been off work today?		

How many points have you won?

Use your English

What are these people saying? There is more than one answer.

Work with a partner and practise the conversations.

Writing

Sergio's teacher has underlined the mistakes in his homework. Rewrite the homework. Correct the underlined mistakes. Add any words and punctuation which are missing (✐ means something is missing).

I usually <u>every summer go to the USA</u>. However, this year
<u>i</u> went to <u>the</u> Greece <u>so</u> <u>i</u> wanted to see my friend <u>a</u>ndreas.
Andreas looked very well. ✐ <u>its</u> great to see you ✐ he said. ✐
Are you com<u>e</u>ing to ✐ Acropolis this evening?
<u>its</u> beautiful at night. ✐
<u>Although</u>, I told <u>he</u> I was a little tired. ✐ <u>Lets</u> go tomorrow,
✐ I said.
<u>a</u>ndreas looked disappointed <u>because</u> I changed my mind.
We went out and had a very happy evening.

LEARNING REVIEW

a) Which of these do you read or listen to in English outside the classroom?

Which is the most useful? Why? Which is the most difficult? Why?

b) Which of these are true for you outside the classroom?

- I look back at my vocabulary notes.
- I practise new words in sentences.
- I look at my grammar notes.
- I read the *Language reference* sections at the end of each Unit.

c) How much more practice do you need in these? Number them 1-7 (1 = I need the most practice).

- listening __
- speaking __
- reading __
- writing __
- grammar __
- vocabulary __
- pronunciation __

Additional material

Unit 3 (page 23)

STUDENT A

a) You are a shop assistant in a clothes shop. Look at your rolecard and think about what you are going to say.

> ROLECARD
> You are helping a customer to buy some new clothes. Think about questions to ask him/her. Examples:
> *What size are you? What colour would you like? Would you like to try it/them on? Does it/Do they fit?*
> Answer the customer's questions. Tell him/her the prices of the clothes and how to pay – cash, credit card or cheque.

b) Have a conversation with your partner.

Unit 3 (page 23)

STUDENT A

Look at the picture below. You and your partner have similar pictures but there are six differences. Take turns to talk about your pictures. When you find a difference you should both write it down.
Example:
A: *In my picture the baby is crying.*
B: *In my picture the baby is sleeping.*
Now find five more differences.

Unit 4 (page 24)

> STUDENT A
> 1 You have got two tickets for a pop concert next Friday evening, 22 July, but your friend is ill and you don't want to go without him/her. Phone the ticket agency and ask if you can have your money back.
> 2 A friend phones you to invite you to dinner. Accept, and ask the person to pick you up in their car.

Unit 4 (page 29)

a) STUDENT A: Look at this puzzle.

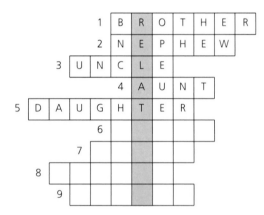

Tell Student B about 2-5. Don't say the words. Tell him/her *about* the words. Example:
1 *Not your sister* = BROTHER

b) Now your partner will tell you about 6-9.
c) Which word can you see in the pink box?

Unit 12 (page 75)

GROUP A: 1 opera   2 Rome   3 Malay, Chinese, Tamil and English   4 at an American university in Cambridge, Mass.

GROUP B: 1 tennis   2 works of art (paintings and sculpture)   3 on a beach in Rio de Janeiro, Brazil   4 play it – it's a Russian musical instrument

Unit 5 (page 30)

STUDENT A
1 You want to go to Chesterfield by train from London.
Ask about the journey: what time/trains? how much/cost?
which platform? how long? last train?
2 You work at Heathrow airport. Answer your partner's
questions.
The flight is one hour late. It leaves from Gate Number 16.
It is boarding at 4.20 am.

Unit 6 (page 39)

STUDENT A
You and your partner have similar pictures. Ask and answer
questions to find the ten differences. Example:
A: *Have you got a lot of rice?*   B: *No, I've only got a little.*

Unit 8 (page 52)

Are you a workaholic? Check your score!

1 (a) 2   (b) 1   (c) 0   6 (a) 2   (b) 0   (c) 1
2 (a) 3   (b) 2   (c) 1   (d) 0   7 (a) 2   (b) 1   (c) 0
3 (a) 2   (b) 0   8 (a) 2   (b) 0
4 (a) 2   (b) 1   (c) 0   9 (a) 2   (b) 0
5 (a) 2   (b) 1   (c) 0

What your score means...

 0-2 You obviously hate work!
 3-6 You take things very easily.
 7-10 You have a good balance between work and fun.
11-14 You work hard. Make sure your health doesn't suffer.
15-19 You are very ambitious. Remember – all work and no play makes
       Jack a dull boy!

Unit 10 (page 60)

Quiz answers

1 b)   5 c)   9 c)   13 b)
2 c)   6 b)   10 c)   14 b)
3 c)   7 c)   11 c)   15 a)
4 a)   8 b)   12 d)

Unit 14 (page 87)

STUDENT A
You and your partner both have
information about Keanu Reeves.
Most of the information is the
same, but you've got some
information which your partner
hasn't got. Use question tags to
check and find the extra
information. Example:
A: *He was born in 1965, wasn't he?*
B: *Yes, he was.*

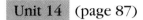

KEANU REEVES

was born in Beirut in 1965. His mother is
English. When he was young he wanted to be
a racing driver. Keanu began acting when he
was 18. He has played in the films *Dracula*
and *Little Buddha*. Keanu loves riding
motorbikes. He has got a 1974 Norton and
drives at 130 mph.

Unit 16 (pages 99 and 130)

Answers to quiz

GROUP A
1 McDonald's restaurants
2 the Portuguese
3 1945
4 J.L. Baird
5 rice
6 Norway

GROUP B
1 1953
2 31 October
3 The USA
4 Memphis
5 Shakespeare
6 France

Unit 4 (page 24)

STUDENT B

1 You work at a ticket agency. Tell people who phone that you can't give them their money back if they want to return their tickets. Offer to sell the tickets for them on the night of the concert.

2 Phone a friend to ask him/her to dinner at a local restaurant. Decide on the day and time. The problem is that your car is at the garage so ask him/her to meet you outside the restaurant.

Unit 5 (page 30)

STUDENT B

1 You work in a railway information office in London. Give your partner the information he/she needs.
Trains to Chesterfield from London are at ten to and twenty past each hour. The journey takes around one hour. The last train to Chesterfield leaves at 11.35. It arrives at 12.40.
A day return ticket is £9.50 if you leave after 9.15 am. If not, it's £14. The Chesterfield train leaves from Platform 4.

2 You want information about your flight to New York. Ask about the boarding time?/gate? on time?

Unit 6 (page 39)

STUDENT B
You and your partner have similar pictures. Ask and answer questions to find the ten differences. Example:
B: *Have you got a little rice?*   A: *No, I've got a lot of rice.*

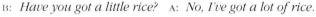

Unit 10 (page 64)

Noughts and crosses questions

Shopping
1 Where do you go to book a holiday?
2 What do you do at a library?
3 Where can you buy a necklace?
4 Where can you buy cough medicine?
5 Where can you buy bread?
6 What is the name for things you take back from holiday (for presents or to help you remember the place)?

Countries/nationalities
1 In which country is Ankara?
2 What language do people speak in Brazil?
3 What nationality was Tolstoy?
4 In which country is the Acropolis?
5 What language do they speak in Corsica?
6 Which country has the airline *Lufthansa*?

Clothes
1 Name four things you wear outside in cold weather.
2 Name three things you wear at bedtime.
3 Where do you try on clothes?
4 Name three things you wear on your feet.
5 What is the name for a jacket and trousers of the same material?
6 10, 12, 14 (or 34, 36, 38) are different _____.

Travel/transport
1 Before you get on a plane you show your ticket and get a _____ card.
2 A general name for suitcases and bags is _____.
3 If your car stops working, it b_____ d_____.
4 A 'room' on a train is called a _____.
5 Name two things you can ride.
6 If you don't catch your bus, you _____ it.

Family
1 Your mother and father are your _____.
2 If your brother gets married, his wife is your _____.
3 Your cousin is your _____.
4 You brother's/sister's daughter is your _____.
5 If a marriage finishes, you get _____.
6 You step-father is your _____.

Food/restaurants
1 Could I have a _____ of bread, please?
2 What is the name of the money you leave the waiter/waitress for their service?
3 Name five vegetables.
4 Name five fruits.
5 Name four different ways of cooking (verbs).

The body/health
1 To lose weight many people go on a _____.
2 What is the opposite of *lose* weight?
3 You have 8 fingers and 2 _____.
4 You wear a watch on your _____.
5 What is the name of the ten things on your feet?
6 Name three things you do or have if you've got a cold.

Homes
1 Name four different kinds of houses.
2 You wash your clothes in a _____.
3 To dry yourself you use a _____.
4 Name five things you put on the table when you are setting it for a meal.
5 Name four different places where people have their homes.
6 Who do you see if you want to buy a house?

Jobs
1 Name three things that are delivered to your house in Britain.
2 What's the name of a person who repairs your car?
3 What's the name of a person who designs buildings?
4 What's another way of saying, 'What's your job?' ?
5 If you lose your job, you are _____.
6 If you see an advert for a job you want, you send for the _____ form.

 **Unit 11** (page 68)

Quiz answers
1 cheetah 3 giraffe 5 giraffe
2 rhino   4 elephant

Unit 12 (page 77)

STUDENT A
Look at the picture above. You are going to ask your partner five questions about the people.
First write your questions. Example:
Is Henry older than Susan?

a) Show your partner your picture. Ask him/her your questions.
b) Compare the people in the two pictures. Example:
I think Helen is the most attractive.

Unit 14 (page 89)

STUDENT A

a) You and your partner have similar pictures. Ask questions and find ten differences. Don't look at your partner's picture and don't show him/her your picture.

b) Now look at your partner's picture and answer these questions.

1 What does the woman look like?
2 What kind of person do you think she is?
3 Where is she?
4 What is happening in the picture?

Unit 16 (page 99)

GROUP A

Look at the quiz below. Write full questions for 4-6.

1 What was introduced into Russia on 2 March 1988? Mobile phones, McDonald's restaurants or credit cards?
2 Who was Brazil controlled by between 1500 and 1825? The Portuguese, the Spanish or the French?
3 When was the United Nations started? 1918, 1938 or 1945?
4 Who/television invented by? G. Marconi, J.L. Baird or A. Bell?
5 What/Japanese drink sake/made from? Potatoes, rice or apples?
6 Where/Winter Olympics/held in 1994? Norway, Canada or Sweden?

Answer all the questions.
Check the answers on page 127.

2 Ask the other group your questions. The group with the most correct answers wins.

Unit 10 (page 64)

Answers to noughts and crosses questions

Shopping
1 a travel agent's   4 a chemist's
2 borrow books   5 a baker's
3 a jeweller's   6 souvenirs

Countries and nationalities
1 Turkey   4 Greece
2 Portuguese   5 French
3 Russian   6 Germany

Clothes
1 scarf, hat, coat, gloves etc.
2 pyjamas, slippers, dressing-gown etc.
3 a changing room
4 sandals, boots, shoes etc.
5 a suit
6 sizes

Travel/transport
1 boarding
2 luggage
3 breaks down
4 carriage/compartment
5 bicycle, horse, tandem etc.
6 miss

Family
1 parents
2 sister-in-law
3 uncle's or aunt's child
4 niece
5 divorced
6 mother's new husband

Food/restaurants
1 loaf
2 tip
3 potatoes, green beans, mushrooms, asparagus, artichokes etc.
4 oranges, pineapples, bananas, apples, grapes etc.
5 grill, roast, bake, fry etc.

The body/health
1 diet
2 *put on* weight
3 thumbs
4 wrist
5 toes
6 you sneeze, you cough, you have a sore throat etc.

Homes
1 farmhouse, bungalow, flat, terraced house etc.
2 washing machine
3 towel
4 knife, fork, spoon, glass, plate etc.
5 city centre, countryside, near the sea, just outside the town
6 an estate agent

Jobs
1 milk, newspapers, letters
2 a mechanic
3 an architect
4 'What do you do?'
5 unemployed
6 application

Unit 16   (page 100)

GROUP A

Look at the picture below. What do you think has happened? What is going to happen?

Now work with a partner from Group B. Listen while your partner tells his/her part of the story. Don't look at your partner's picture. Then tell the story in your picture.

Unit 17   (page 107)

STUDENT A

a) What are the past participles of these verbs: write, see, be, buy, shut, teach, read, do, catch, eat?

b) Your partner is going to ask you about some past participles.

c) Ask your partner about the past participles of your verbs. Write down his/her answers. Don't say if the answer is correct or not. Example:
  A: *What is the past participle of write?*
  B: *Written.*

d) Check your answers on page 132. Who got the most correct answers?

Unit 18   (page 111)

STUDENT A
You are from the same family as Student B. Choose how you are related. Are you husband and wife, brother and sister or parent and child? You have had an argument. You are angry with Student B because he/she:

- gets up late
- doesn't help in the house
- borrows a lot of money

Make a list of other things you are angry about (money, parties, TV, clothes, car etc.) You aren't speaking to Student B but Student C is a go-between. Ask him/her to help you.

Unit 20   (page 120)

STUDENT A
You are going to book into the Swan Hotel for two weeks. It's very important that this holiday goes well and everything is right for you. What information do you want about the hotel? Student A is the hotel's receptionist. Ask him/her questions about: park/car? how far/city centre?/TV? rooms with private bathrooms? central heating? restaurant? bring/dog? price?

Pronunciation: phonemic chart

CONSONANTS				VOWELS		DIPHTHONGS	
symbol	key word	symbol	key word	symbol	key word	symbol	key word
/ p /	**p**en	/ s /	**s**oon	/ iː /	s**ee**	/ eɪ /	m**a**k**e**
/ b /	**b**ack	/ z /	**z**oo	/ ɪ /	h**i**m	/ əʊ /	n**o**
/ t /	**t**ea	/ ʃ /	fi**sh**	/ e /	b**e**d	/ aɪ /	wr**i**t**e**
/ d /	**d**ay	/ ʒ /	televi**s**ion	/ æ /	b**a**d	/ aʊ /	n**ow**
/ k /	**k**ey	/ h /	**h**ot	/ ɑː /	c**ar**	/ ɔɪ /	b**oy**
/ g /	**g**et	/ m /	**c**ome	/ ɒ /	h**o**t	/ ɪə /	h**ere**
/ tʃ /	**ch**air	/ n /	su**n**	/ ɔː /	s**aw**	/ eə /	th**ere**
/ dʒ /	**j**ump	/ ŋ /	E**ng**lish	/ ʊ /	p**u**t	/ ʊə /	t**our**
/ f /	**f**at	/ l /	**l**amp	/ uː /	y**ou**		
/ v /	**v**ery	/ r /	**r**ed	/ ʌ /	c**u**t		
/ θ /	**th**ing	/ j /	**y**et	/ ɜː /	b**ir**d		
/ ð /	**th**en	/ w /	**w**et	/ ə /	Chin**a**		

Irregular verbs

VERB	PAST SIMPLE	PAST PARTICIPLE	VERB	PAST SIMPLE	PAST PARTICIPLE
be	was/were	been	leave	left	left
become	became	become	lend	lent	lent
begin	began	begun	lose	lost	lost
blow	blew	blown	make	made	made
break	broke	broken	mean	meant	meant
bring	brought	brought	meet	met	met
build	built	built	pay	paid	paid
burn	burned, burnt	burned, burnt	put	put	put
buy	bought	bought	read	read	read
catch	caught	caught	ride	rode	ridden
choose	chose	chosen	ring	rang	rung
come	came	come	run	ran	run
cost	cost	cost	say	said	said
cut	cut	cut	see	saw	seen
do	did	done	sell	sold	sold
draw	drew	drawn	send	sent	sent
dream	dreamed, dreamt	dreamed, dreamt	shake	shook	shaken
drink	drank	drunk	show	showed	shown, showed
drive	drove	driven	shut	shut	shut
eat	ate	eaten	sing	sang	sung
fall	fell	fallen	sit	sat	sat
feed	fed	fed	sleep	slept	slept
feel	felt	felt	speak	spoke	spoken
find	found	found	spell	spelt	spelt
fly	flew	flown	spend	spent	spent
forget	forgot	forgotten	stand	stood	stood
freeze	froze	frozen	steal	stole	stolen
get	got	got	swim	swam	swum
give	gave	given	take	took	taken
go	went	gone, been	teach	taught	taught
grow	grew	grown	tell	told	told
have	had	had	think	thought	thought
hear	heard	heard	throw	threw	thrown
hide	hid	hidden	understand	understood	understood
hit	hit	hit	wake	woke	woken
held	held	held	wear	wore	worn
keep	kept	kept	win	won	won
know	knew	known	write	wrote	written
learn	learned, learnt	learned, learnt			

Word list

This is a list of the most useful new words in each unit. *n* = noun *v* = verb *adj* = adjective *adv* = adverb

UNIT 1

advice *(n)* /əd'vaɪs/
afraid *(adj)* (*I'm afraid not*) /ə'freɪd/
amazing *(adj)* /ə'meɪzɪŋ/
belong (to) *(v)* /bɪ'lɒŋ/
biscuit *(n)* /'bɪskɪt/
board *(n)* (*on the board*) /bɔːd/
boot *(n)* /buːt/
brain *(n)* /breɪn/
capital *(n)* /'kæpɪtl/
champion *(n)* /'tʃæmpiən/
connect *(v)* /kə'nekt/
cycle *(n)* /'saɪkəl/
earn *(v)* /ɜːn/
elderly *(adj)* /'eldəli/
engaged *(adj)* (*to be engaged*)
    /'ɪn'ɡeɪdʒd/
engineer *(n)* /ˌendʒɪ'nɪə/
enjoy *(v)* /ɪn'dʒɔɪ/
exercise *(n)* (*to take exercise*) /'eksəsaɪz/
exercise *(v)* /'eksəsaɪz/
experience *(n)* /ɪk'spɪəriəns/
famous *(adj)* /'feɪməs/
favourite *(adj)* /'feɪvərɪt/
film *(n)* /fɪlm/
imagine *(v)* /ɪ'mædʒɪn/
improve *(v)* /ɪm'pruːv/
introduce *(v)* /ˌɪntrə'djuːs/
invitation *(n)* /ˌɪnvɪ'teɪʃən/
invite *(v)* /ɪn'vaɪt/
list *(n)* /lɪst/
lovely *(adj)* /'lʌvli/
magazine *(n)* /ˌmæɡə'ziːn/
matter *(v)* (*it doesn't matter*) /'mætə/
memory *(n)* /'meməri/
mind *(n)* /maɪnd/
picture *(n)* /'pɪktʃə/
pleased *(adj)* (*pleased to meet you*)
    /pliːzd/
polite *(adj)* /pə'laɪt/
practise *(v)* /'præktɪs/
remember *(v)* /rɪ'membə/
remind *(v)* /rɪ'maɪnd/
rub out *(v)* /rʌb 'aʊt/
rude *(adj)* /ruːd/
shape *(n)* /ʃeɪp/
success *(n)* /sək'ses/

UNIT 2

baker's *(n)* /'beɪkəz/
bite *(v)* /baɪt/
boss *(n)* /bɒs/
bright *(adj)* /braɪt/
businessman *(n)* /'bɪznɪsmən/
butcher's *(n)* /'bʊtʃəz/
café *(n)* /'kæfeɪ/
casual *(adj)* /'kæʒʊəl/
certainly *(adv)* /'sɜːtnli/
changing room *(n)* /'tʃeɪndʒɪŋ ruːm/
chemist's *(n)* /'kemɪsts/
cheque (*traveller's cheque*) *(n)* /tʃek/

collect *(v)* /kə'lekt/
comfortable *(adj)* /'kʌmftəbəl/
cottage *(n)* /'kɒtɪdʒ/
dress *(n)* /dres/
earring *(n)* /'ɪəˌrɪŋ/
enormous *(adj)* /ɪ'nɔːməs/
expensive *(adj)* /ɪk'spensɪv/
fit *(adj)* (=healthy) /fɪt/
greengrocer's *(n)* /'ɡriːnˌɡrəʊsəz/
jacket *(n)* /'dʒækɪt/
jeweller's *(n)* /'dʒuːələz/
jewellery *(n)* /'dʒuːəlri/
jumper *(n)* /'dʒʌmpə/
leggings *(n)* /'leɡɪŋz/
lip *(n)* /lɪp/
loaf *(n)* /ləʊf/
necklace *(n)* /'nek-lɪs/
nervous *(adj)* /'nɜːvəs/
pet *(n)* /pet/
photography *(n)* /fə'tɒɡrəfi/
plant pot *(n)* /plɑːnt pɒt/
popular *(adj)* /'pɒpjələ/
pyjamas *(n)* /pə'dʒɑːməz/
sale *(n)* /seɪl/
save *(v)* /seɪv/
sell out *(v)* /sel 'aʊt/
sign *(v)* /saɪn/
size *(n)* /saɪz/
skirt *(n)* /skɜːt/
smart *(adj)* /smɑːt/
souvenir *(n)* /ˌsuːvə'nɪə/
spare *(adj)* (*spare time*) /speə/
suit *(n)* /suːt/
sweatshirt *(n)* /'swet-ʃɜːt/
T-shirt *(n)* /'tiːʃɜːt/
tidy *(adj)* /'taɪdi/
tie *(n)* /taɪ/
track-suit *(n)* /'træk suːt/
traditional *(adj)* /trə'dɪʃənəl/
trainers *(n)* /'treɪnəs/
traveller *(n)* (*traveller's cheques*)
    /'trævələ/
try on *(v)* /traɪ ɒn/
watch strap *(n)* /'wɒtʃstræp/

UNIT 3

affectionate *(adj)* /ə'fekʃənət/
age *(n)* /eɪdʒ/
alarm clock *(n)* /ə'lɑːm klɒk/
alone *(adj)* /ə'ləʊn/
ambitious *(adj)* /æm'bɪʃəs/
attractive *(adj)* /ə'træktɪv/
brother-in-law *(n)* /'brʌðəɪnˌlɔː/
build *(v)* /bɪld/
busy *(adj)* /'bɪzi/
calm *(adj)* /kɑːm/
cash *(n)* /kæʃ/
close (to) *(adj)* /kləʊz (tə) /
cousin *(n)* /'kʌzən/
credit card *(n)* /'kredɪt kɑːd/
cry *(v)* /kraɪ/
customer *(n)* /'kʌstəmə/

dark *(adj)* (*dark hair/eyes*) /dɑːk/
different *(adj)* /'dɪfərənt/
divorced *(adj)* /dɪ'vɔːst/
dressing gown *(n)* /'dresɪŋ ɡaʊn/
easygoing *(adj)* /ˌiːzi'ɡəʊɪŋ/
energetic *(adj)* /ˌenə'dʒetɪk/
extravagant *(adj)* /ɪk'strævəɡənt/
fail *(v)* /feɪl/
fashion *(n)* /'fæʃən/
feel *(v)* /fiːl/
fight *(n)* /faɪt/
friendly *(adj)* /'frendli/
fun *(n)* /fʌn/
funny *(adj)* /'fʌni/
generous *(adj)* /'dʒenərəs/
get on with *(v)* /ɡet 'ɒn wɪð/
good-tempered *(adj)* /ɡʊd 'tempəd/
grandparent *(n)* /'ɡrænˌpeərənt/
hit *(v)* /hɪt/
honest *(adj)* /'ɒnɪst/
immature *(adj)* /ˌɪmə'tʃʊə/
independent *(adj)* /ˌɪndɪ'pendənt/
interested *(adj)* /'ɪntrəstɪd/
interesting *(adj)* /'ɪntrəstɪŋ/
lies *(n)* (*to tell lies*) /laɪz/
lively *(adj)* /'laɪvli/
look like *(v)* /'lʊk laɪk/
manage *(v)* (*to manage a hotel*)
    /'mænɪdʒ/
middle-aged *(adj)* /'mɪdl'eɪdʒd/
model *(n)* /'mɒdl/
motorway *(n)* /'məʊtəweɪ/
nephew *(n)* /'nefjuː/
niece *(n)* /niːs/
normal *(adj)* /'nɔːməl/
parent *(n)* /'peərənt/
patient *(adj)* /'peɪʃənt/
personality *(n)* /pɜːsə'næliti/
plate *(n)* /pleɪt/
poster *(n)* /'pəʊstə/
postman *(n)* /'pəʊstmən/
relation *(n)* /rɪ'leɪʃən/
relaxed *(adj)* /rɪ'lækst/
relaxing *(adj)* /rɪ'læksɪŋ/
rip up *(v)* /rɪp 'ʌp/
silly *(adj)* /'sɪli/
stepfather *(n)* /'stepˌfɑːðə/
strict *(adj)* /strɪkt/
succeed *(v)* /sək'siːd/
take after *(v)* /teɪk 'ɑːftə/
thoughtless *(adj)* /'θɔːtləs/
twins *(n)* /twɪnz/
uncle *(n)* /'ʌŋkəl/
unusual *(adj)* /ʌn'juːʒʊəl/
wedding *(n)* /'wedɪŋ/

UNIT 4

accident *(n)* /'æksɪdənt/
advertisement *(n)* /əd'vɜːtɪsmənt/
afford *(v)* (*I can't afford*) /ə'fɔːd/
ankle *(n)* /'æŋkəl/
army *(n)* /'ɑːmi/

aspirin *(n)* /ˈæsprɪn/
awful *(adj)* /ˈɔːfəl/
book *(v)* *(to **book** a hotel)* /bʊk/
careful *(adj)* /ˈkeəfəl/
check *(v)* /tʃek/
chest *(n)* /tʃest/
cold *(n)* *(I've got a **cold**)* /kəʊld/
cough *(n)* /kɒf/
cut down on *(v)* /kʌt ˈdaʊn ɒn/
dangerous *(adj)* /ˈdeɪndʒrəs/
delicious *(adj)* /dɪˈlɪʃəs/
diet *(n)* *(to go on a **diet**)* /ˈdaɪət/
flu *(n)* /fluː/
give up *(v)* /gɪv ʌp/
hairdresser's *(n)* /ˈheəˌdresəz/
hang on *(v)* /hæŋ ˈɒn/
headache *(n)* /ˈhedeɪk/
healthy *(adj)* /ˈhelθi/
hire *(v)* /haɪə/
illness *(n)* /ˈɪlnəs/
lie down *(v)* /laɪ ˈdaʊn/
luggage *(n)* /ˈlʌgɪdʒ/
medicine *(n)* /ˈmedsən/
rest *(v)* /rest/
sick *(adj)* *(to feel **sick**)* /sɪk/
snack *(n)* /snæk/
sneeze *(v)* /sniːz/
sore *(adj)* *(**sore** throat)* /sɔː/
sprain *(v)* /spreɪn/
stomach *(n)* /ˈstʌmək/
stomachache *(n)* /ˈstʌmək-eɪk/
swollen *(adj)* /ˈswəʊlən/
tap *(n)* /tæp/
throat *(n)* /θrəʊt/
train *(n)* /treɪn/
travel agent *(n)* /ˈtrævəl ˌeɪdʒənt/
twisted *(adj)* /ˈtwɪstɪd/
visa *(n)* /ˈviːzə/
weight *(n)* *(to put on/lose **weight**)* /weɪt/

UNIT 5

arrangements *(n)* *(to make
  arrangements)* /əˈreɪndʒməntz/
boarding card *(n)* /ˈbɔːdɪŋ kɑːd/
break down *(v)* /breɪk ˈdaʊn/
can't stand *(v)* /kɑːnt ˈstænd/
change *(n)* /tʃeɪndʒ/
change *(v)* /tʃeɪndʒ/
check in *(v)* /tʃek ˈɪn/
confirm *(v)* *(to **confirm** a flight)*
  /kənˈfɜːm/
couple *(n)* /ˈkʌpəl/
day return *(adj)* /ˌdeɪ rɪˈtɜːn/
exciting *(adj)* /ɪkˈsaɪtɪŋ/
fall *(v)* /fɔːl/
fine *(adj)* /faɪn/
fine *(n)* /faɪn/
fingers *(n)* /ˈfɪŋgəz/
garage *(n)* /ˈgærɑːʒ/
get into *(v)* /get ˈɪntə/
get off *(v)* /get ˈɒf/
get on *(v)* /get ˈɒn/
get out of *(v)* /get ˈaʊt əv/
lean *(v)* /liːn/
lift *(n)* /lɪft/
lorry *(n)* /ˈlɒri/
mind *(v)* *(I don't **mind**)* /maɪnd/
miss *(v)* *(to **miss** a bus)* /mɪs/
petrol *(n)* /ˈpetrəl/
platform *(n)* /ˈplætfɔːm/

railway station *(n)* /ˈreɪlweɪ ˌsteɪʃən/
realise *(v)* /ˈrɪəlaɪz/
reliable *(adj)* /rɪˈlaɪəbəl/
reserve *(v)* /rɪˈzɜːv/
romantic *(adj)* /rəʊˈmæntɪk/
safe *(adj)* /seɪf/
service station *(n)* /ˈsɜːvɪs ˌsteɪʃən/
single *(adj)* *(**single** or return)* /ˈsɪŋgəl/
surprise *(n)* /səˈpraɪz/
thumb *(n)* /θʌm/
transport *(n)* /ˈtrænspɔːt/
trip *(n)* /trɪp/
trip *(v)* /trɪp/
waist *(n)* /weɪst/
wrist *(n)* /rɪst/

UNIT 6

art gallery *(n)* /ɑːt ˈgæləri/
asparagus *(n)* /əˈspærəgəs/
bake *(v)* /beɪk/
beach *(n)* /biːtʃ/
beef *(n)* /biːf/
bill *(n)* /bɪl/
boil *(v)* /bɔɪl/
break *(v)* /breɪk/
cassette *(n)* /kəˈset/
chop *(n)* /tʃɒp/
coast *(n)* /kəʊst/
cod *(n)* /kɒd/
crab *(n)* /kræb/
dessert *(n)* /dɪˈzɜːt/
dressing *(n)* /ˈdresɪŋ/
fork *(n)* /fɔːk/
fried *(adj)* /fraɪd/
fry *(v)* /fraɪ/
frying-pan *(n)* /ˈfraɪŋˌpæn/
grill *(n)* /grɪl/
grill *(v)* /grɪl/
grilled *(adj)* /grɪld/
honey *(n)* /ˈhʌni/
journey *(n)* /ˈdʒɜːni/
knife *(n)* /naɪf/
lamb *(n)* /læm/
lettuce *(n)* /ˈletɪs/
main course *(n)* /meɪn kɔːs/
mushroom *(n)* /ˈmʌʃruːm/
napkin *(n)* /ˈnæpkɪn/
oven *(n)* /ˈʌvən/
pack *(v)* /pæk/
peppers *(n)* /ˈpepəz/
pineapple *(n)* /ˈpaɪnæpəl/
plaice *(n)* /pleɪs/
plain *(adj)* /pleɪn/
prawn *(n)* /prɔːn/
pudding *(n)* /ˈpʊdɪŋ/
roast *(n)* /rəʊst/
run out of *(v)* /rʌn ˈaʊt əv/
sauce *(n)* /sɔːs/
saucepan *(n)* /ˈsɔːspæn/
service *(n)* /ˈsɜːvɪs/
set *(v)* *(to **set** the table)* /set/
shell *(n)* /ʃel/
snail *(n)* /sneɪl/
spicy *(adj)* /ˈspaɪsi/
spoon *(n)* /spuːn/
starter *(n)* /ˈstɑːtə/
starving *(v)* *(I'm **starving**)* /ˈstɑːvɪŋ/
suck *(v)* /sʌk/
suitcase *(n)* /ˈsuːtkeɪs/
tip *(n)* /tɪp/

waiter *(n)* /ˈweɪtə/
waitress *(n)* /ˈweɪtrəs/
wildlife *(n)* /ˈwaɪldlaɪf/
writing paper *(n)* /ˈraɪtɪŋ ˌpeɪpə/
yoghurt *(n)* /ˈjɒgət/

UNIT 7

annoyed *(adj)* /əˈnɔɪd/
argue *(v)* /ˈɑːgjuː/
bored *(adj)* /bɔːd/
boring *(adj)* /ˈbɔːrɪŋ/
borrow *(v)* /ˈbɒrəʊ/
carpet *(n)* /ˈkɑːpɪt/
curtains *(n)* /ˈkɜːtnz/
depressed *(adj)* /dɪˈprest/
depressing *(adj)* /dɪˈpresɪŋ/
dreadful *(adj)* /ˈdredfəl/
embarrassed *(adj)* /ɪmˈbærəst/
embarrassing *(adj)* /ɪmˈbærəsɪŋ/
environment *(n)* /ɪnˈvaɪrənmənt/
excited *(adj)* /ɪkˈsaɪtɪd/
fed up *(adj)* *(He's **fed up** with me)* /ˌfed
  ˈʌp/
frightened *(adj)* /ˈfraɪtnd/
frightening *(adj)* /ˈfraɪtnɪŋ/
furniture *(n)* /ˈfɜːnɪtʃə/
great *(adj)* /greɪt/
headline *(n)* /ˈhedlaɪn/
kids *(n)* /kɪdz/
lay *(v)* *(to **lay** the carpet)* /leɪ/
move in *(v)* /muːv ɪn/
news *(n)* /njuːz/
novel *(n)* /ˈnɒvəl/
paint *(v)* /peɪnt/
pick up *(v)* /pɪk ˈʌp/
politics *(n)* /ˈpɒlɪtɪks/
prize *(n)* /praɪz/
second-hand *(adj)* /ˌsekənˈhænd/
shelf *(n)* /ʃelf/
sitting room *(n)* /ˈsɪtɪŋ ruːm/
surprised *(adj)* /səˈpraɪzd/
surprising *(adj)* /səˈpraɪzɪŋ/
tiring *(adj)* /ˈtaɪrɪŋ/
vegetarian *(n)* /ˌvedʒɪˈteəriən/
wonderful *(adj)* /ˈwʌndəfəl/
worried *(adj)* /ˈwʌrɪd/
worry *(v)* /ˈwʌri/

UNIT 8

actor *(n)* /ˈæktə/
accountant *(n)* /əˈkaʊntənt/
application form *(n)* /ˌæplɪˈkeɪʃən fɔːm/
architect *(n)* /ˈɑːkɪtekt/
cheerful *(adj)* /ˈtʃɪəfəl/
comedy *(n)* /ˈkɒmədi/
delighted *(adj)* /dɪˈlaɪtɪd/
deliver *(v)* /dɪˈlɪvə/
discover *(v)* /dɪsˈkʌvə/
duck *(n)* /dʌk/
dull *(adj)* /dʌl/
entertainment *(n)* /ˌentəˈteɪnmənt/
expect *(v)* /ɪkˈspekt/
fancy *(v)* *(Do you **fancy** . . .?)* /ˈfænsi/
fascinating *(adj)* /ˈfæsɪneɪtɪŋ/
fireworks *(n)* /ˈfaɪəwɜːks/
funeral *(n)* /ˈfjuːnərəl/
funfair *(n)* /ˈfʌnfeə/
huge *(adj)* /hjuːdʒ/
journalist *(n)* /ˈdʒɜːnəlɪst/

keen *(adj) (to be **keen** on)* /kiːn/
librarian *(n)* /laɪˈbreəriən/
light *(adj)* /laɪt/
look after *(v)* /lʊk ˈɑːftə/
manage *(v) (= to succeed)* /ˈmænɪdʒ/
mean *(adj)* /miːn/
mechanic *(n)* /mɪˈkænɪk/
miss *(v) (= feel sorry because someone is absent)* /mɪs/
octopus *(n)* /ˈɒktəpəs/
peel *(v)* /piːl/
politician *(n)* /pɒlɪˈtɪʃən/
post *(v) (to **post** letters)* /pəʊst/
refuse *(v)* /rɪˈfjuːz/
salary *(n)* /ˈsæləri/
shark *(n)* /ʃɑːk/
shrimp *(n)* /ʃrɪmp/
squirrel *(n)* /ˈskwɪrəl/
suggest *(v)* /səˈdʒest/
tunnel *(n)* /ˈtʌnl/

UNIT 9

adult *(n)* /ˈædʌlt/
bedside table *(n)* /ˈbedsaɪd ˈteɪbəl/
bungalow *(n)* /ˈbʌŋgələʊ/
career *(n)* /kəˈrɪə/
cartoon *(n)* /kɑːˈtuːn/
childhood *(n)* /ˈtʃaɪldhʊd/
client *(n)* /ˈklaɪənt/
coffee table *(n)* /ˈkɒfi ˌteɪbəl/
colourful *(adj)* /ˈkʌləfəl/
cooker *(n)* /kʊkə/
countryside *(n)* /ˈkʌntrɪsaɪd/
crash *(n)* /kræʃ/
cuddle *(v)* /ˈkʌdl/
cupboard *(n)* /ˈkʌbəd/
degree *(n) (a university **degree**)* /dɪˈgriː/
dishwasher *(n)* /ˈdɪʃˌwɒʃə/
elect *(v)* /ɪˈlekt/
election *(n)* /ɪˈlekʃən/
employ *(v)* /ɪmˈplɔɪ/
estate agent *(n)* /ɪˈsteɪt ˌeɪdʒənt/
farmhouse *(n)* /ˈfɑːmhaʊs/
freezer *(n)* /ˈfriːzə/
furious *(adj)* /ˈfjʊəriəs/
hurt *(v) (to **hurt** yourself)* /hɜːt/
jealous *(adj)* /ˈdʒeləs/
kettle *(n)* /ˈketl/
knees *(n)* /niːz/
laugh *(v)* /lɑːf/
law *(n)* /lɔː/
luck *(n)* /lʌk/
microwave *(n)* /ˈmaɪkrəweɪv/
mirror *(n)* /ˈmɪrə/
miserable *(adj)* /ˈmɪzrəbəl/
possession *(n)* /pəˈzeʃən/
run *(v) (to **run** the country)* /rʌn/
scream *(v)* /skriːm/
sink *(n)* /sɪŋk/
slippers *(n)* /ˈslɪpəz/
soap *(n)* /səʊp/
spacious *(adj)* /ˈspeɪʃəs/
stir *(v)* /stɜː/
superstition *(n)* /ˌsuːpəˈstɪʃən/
toaster *(n)* /ˈtəʊstə/
towel rail *(n)* /ˈtaʊəl reɪl/
unemployment *(n)* /ˌʌnɪmˈplɔɪmənt/
unimportant *(adj)* /ˌʌnɪmˈpɔːtənt/
vase *(n)* /vɑːz/
washbasin *(n)* /ˈwɒʃˌbeɪsən/

washing machine *(n)* /ˈwɒʃɪŋ məˌʃiːn/
wastepaper basket *(n)* /ˌweɪst ˈpeɪpə ˌbɑːskɪt/
window sill *(n)* /ˈwɪndəʊ ˌsɪl/

UNIT 10

apologise *(v)* /əˈpɒlədʒaɪz/
coin *(n)* /kɔɪn/
conventional *(adj)* /kənˈvenʃənəl/
corridor *(n)* /ˈkɒrɪdɔː/
failure *(n)* /ˈfeɪljə/
foreigner *(n)* /ˈfɒrɪnə/
licence *(n) (driving **licence**)* /ˈlaɪsəns/
prime minister *(n)* /ˌpraɪm ˈmɪnɪstə/
sense of humour *(n)* /sens əv ˈhjuːmə/

UNIT 11

acting *(n)* /ˈæktɪŋ/
bird-watching *(n)* /ˈbɜːd ˌwɒtʃɪŋ/
booking form *(n)* /ˈbʊkɪŋ fɔːm/
breathe *(v)* /briːð/
camping *(n)* /ˈkæmpɪŋ/
car hire *(n)* /kɑː haɪə/
climb *(v)* /klaɪm/
complete *(v)* /kəmˈpliːt/
date of birth *(n)* /ˌdeɪt əv ˈbɜːθ/
departure *(n)* /dɪˈpɑːtʃə/
dive *(n)* /daɪv/
driving licence *(n)* /ˈdraɪvɪŋ ˌlaɪsəns/
elephant *(n)* /ˈelɪfənt/
emotional *(adj)* /ɪˈməʊʃənəl/
fattening *(adj)* /ˈfætnɪŋ/
fill in *(v) (to **fill in** a form)* /fɪl ˈɪn/
giraffe *(n)* /dʒəˈrɑːf/
good-looking *(adj)* /ˌgʊd ˈlʊkɪŋ/
hang-gliding *(n)* /ˈhæŋ ˌglaɪdɪŋ/
hard-working *(adj)* /ˌhɑːd ˈwɜːkɪŋ/
hobby *(n)* /ˈhɒbi/
ice skating *(n)* /ˈaɪs skeɪtɪŋ/
immigration *(n)* /ˌɪmɪˈgreɪʃən/
join *(v) (to **join** a club)* /dʒɔɪn/
knitting *(n)* /ˈnɪtɪŋ/
length *(n)* /leŋθ/
nationality *(n)* /ˌnæʃəˈnælɪti/
neck *(n)* /nek/
parachuting *(n)* /ˈpærəʃuːtɪŋ/
passport *(n)* /ˈpɑːspɔːt/
permanent *(adj)* /ˈpɜːmənənt/
purpose *(n)* /ˈpɜːpəs/
sales manager *(n)* /ˈseɪlz ˌmænɪdʒə/
short-sighted *(adj)* /ˌʃɔːt ˈsaɪtɪd/
signature *(n)* /ˈsɪgnɪtʃə/
snake *(n)* /sneɪk/
sociable *(adj)* /ˈsəʊʃəbəl/
stamp-collecting *(n)* /ˈstæmp kəˌlektɪŋ/
stay *(n)* /steɪ/
surname *(n)* /ˈsɜːneɪm/
tiger *(n)* /ˈtaɪgə/
ugly *(adj)* /ˈʌgli/
waste *(v) (to **waste** time)* /weɪst/
water-skiing *(n)* /ˈwɔːtə ˌskiːɪŋ/

UNIT 12

accept *(v)* /əkˈsept/
argument *(n)* /ˈɑːgjʊmənt/
arrest *(v)* /əˈrest/
burglar *(n)* /ˈbɜːglə/
chilly *(adj)* /ˈtʃɪli/

commit *(v) (to **commit** a crime)* /kəˈmɪt/
competition *(n)* /ˌkɒmpəˈtɪʃən/
confess *(v)* /kənˈfes/
crime *(n)* /kraɪm/
dial *(v)* /daɪəl/
evidence *(n)* /ˈevɪdəns/
explanation *(n)* /ˌekspləˈneɪʃən/
fall in love *(v)* /ˌfɔːl ɪn ˈlʌv/
freezing *(adj)* /ˈfriːzɪŋ/
horrified *(adj)* /ˈhɒrɪfaɪd/
improvement *(n)* /ɪmˈpruːvmənt/
judge *(n)* /dʒʌdʒ/
microphone *(n)* /ˈmaɪkrəfəʊn/
neighbour *(n)* /ˈneɪbə/
opinion *(n)* /əˈpɪnjən/
postcard *(n)* /ˈpəʊstkɑːd/
prison *(n)* /ˈprɪzən/
record *(v)* /rɪˈkɔːd/
robber *(n)* /ˈrɒbə/
saving *(n)* /ˈseɪvɪŋ/
steal *(v)* /stiːl/
thief *(n)* /θiːf/
towel *(n)* /ˈtaʊəl/
upset *(adj)* /ʌpˈset/
voice *(n)* /vɔɪs/
warning *(n)* /ˈwɔːnɪŋ/
witness *(n)* /ˈwɪtnɪs/

UNIT 13

adore *(v)* /əˈdɔː/
bad-tempered *(adj)* /bæd ˈtempəd/
be fond of *(v)* /bi ˈfɒnd əv/
blanket *(n)* /ˈblæŋkɪt/
buggy *(n)* /ˈbʌgi/
clever *(adj)* /ˈklevə/
corkscrew *(n)* /ˈkɔːkskruː/
crossroads *(n)* /ˈkrɒsrəʊdz/
depend *(v)* /dɪˈpend/
dream *(v)* /driːm/
garlic *(n)* /ˈgɑːlɪk/
get married *(v)* /get ˈmærɪd/
get pregnant *(v)* /get ˈpregnənt/
glue *(n)* /gluː/
go out together *(v)* /gəʊ ˌaʊt təˈgeðə/
interview *(v)* /ˈɪntəvjuː/
lazy *(adj)* /ˈleɪzi/
leather *(adj)* /ˈleðə/
marriage *(n)* /ˈmærɪdʒ/
old-fashioned *(adj)* /ˌəʊld ˈfæʃənd/
one-way street *(n)* /ˌwʌn ˈweɪ ˌstriːt/
patient *(adj)* /ˈpeɪʃənt/
pedestrian crossing *(n)* /pəˌdestriən ˈkrɒsɪŋ/
perfect *(adj)* /ˈpɜːfɪkt/
purse *(n)* /pɜːs/
roundabout *(n)* /ˈraʊndəbaʊt/
scarf *(n)* /skɑːf/
scissors *(n)* /ˈsɪzəz/
shoplift *(v)* /ˈʃɒplɪft/
shy *(adj)* /ʃaɪ/
straight *(adj) (**straight** on)* /streɪt/
T-junction *(n)* /ˈtiː ˌdʒʌŋkʃən/
talkative *(adj)* /ˈtɔːkətɪv/
traffic lights *(n)* /ˈtræfɪk laɪts/
unnatural *(adj)* /ʌnˈnætʃərəl/
vacuum cleaner *(n)* /ˈvækjuəm ˌkliːnə/
wallet *(n)* /ˈwɒlɪt/
woollen *(adj)* /ˌwʊlən/

UNIT 14

amusing (adj) /ə'mju:zɪŋ/
annual (adj) /'ænjuəl/
artist (n) /'ɑ:tɪst/
audience (n) /'ɔ:diəns/
author (n) /'ɔ:θə/
battery (n) /'bætəri/
behave (v) /bɪ'heɪv/
CD (n) /si:'di:/
circus (n) /'sɜ:kəs/
clap (v) /klæp/
clerk (n) /klɑ:k/
comedian (n) /kə'mi:diən/
composer (n) /kəm'pəʊzə/
concert (n) /'kɒnsət/
conductor (n) /kən'dʌktə/
confident (adj) /'kɒnfɪdənt/
deep (adj) /di:p/
drama (n) /'drɑ:mə/
drawing (n) /'drɔ:ɪŋ/
energy (n) /'enədʒi/
exhibition (n) /ˌeksɪ'bɪʃən/
fan (n) (a pop **fan**) /fæn/
film director (n) /'fɪlm dəˌrektə/
front row (n) /ˌfrʌnt 'rəʊ/
headphones (n) /'hedfəʊnz/
interval (n) /'ɪntəvəl/
kidnap (v) /'kɪdnæp/
loudspeaker (n) /ˌlaʊd'spi:kə/
motorbike (n) /'məʊtəbaɪk/
musician (n) /mju:'zɪʃən/
name (v) (to **name** a baby) /neɪm/
newsagent's (n) /'nju:zˌeɪdʒənts/
nicely (adj) /'naɪsli/
nurse (n) /nɜ:s/
obsession (n) /əb'seʃən/
own (v) (to **own** a shop) /əʊn/
performance (n) /pə'fɔ:məns/
pop group (n) /pɒpgru:p/
racing driver (n) /'reɪsɪŋ ˌdraɪvə/
screen (n) /skri:n/
sculpture (n) /'skʌlptʃə/
shocking (adj) /'ʃɒkɪŋ/
show (n) (to see a **show**) /ʃəʊ/
stage (n) /steɪdʒ/
stereo system (n) /'steriəʊ ˌsɪstəm/
video recorder (n) /'vɪdiəʊ rɪˌkɔ:də/
video tape (n) /'vɪdiəʊ teɪp/
zoo (n) /zu:/

UNIT 15

attend (v) /ə'tend/
crazy (adj) (It's **crazy**) /'kreɪzi/
drugs (n) /drʌgz/
economics (n) /ˌekə'nɒmɪks/
educate (v) /'edjʊkeɪt/
employer (n) /ɪm'plɔɪə/
history (n) /'hɪstri/
inexpensive (adj) /ˌɪnɪk'spensɪv/
IT (information technology) (n) /ˌaɪ 'ti:
    (ˌɪnfə'meɪʃən tek'nɒlədʒi) /
punish (v) /'pʌnɪʃ/
rule (n) /ru:l/
science (n) /'saɪəns/
too (adv) /tu:/
top (n) /tɒp/
typing (n) /'taɪpɪŋ/
uniform (n) /'ju:nɪfɔ:m/

UNIT 16

alive (adj) /ə'laɪv/
assassinate (v) /ə'sæsɪneɪt/
attack (v) /ə'tæk/
best-selling (adj) /ˌbest 'selɪŋ/
blow up(v) (= explode) /bləʊ 'ʌp/
bomb (n) /bɒm/
celebrate (v) /'selɪbreɪt/
cloud (n) /klaʊd/
collapse (v) /kə'læps/
confused (adj) /kən'fju:zd/
cool (adj) /ku:l/
destroy (v) /dɪ'strɔɪ/
dishonest (adj) /dɪs'ɒnɪst/
drunk (adj) /drʌŋk/
earthquake (n) /'ɜ:θkweɪk/
explosion (n) /ɪk'spləʊʒən/
horoscope (n) /'hɒrəskəʊp/
incorrect (adj) /ˌɪnkə'rekt/
invent (v) /ɪn'vent/
light bulb (n) /ˌlaɪt bʌlb/
nonsense (n) /'nɒnsəns/
nonstop (adj) /ˌnɒn 'stɒp/
nonstop (adv) /ˌnɒn 'stɒp/
organise (v) /'ɔ:gənaɪz/
question (v) (to **question** somebody)
    /'kwestʃən/
razor blade (n) /'reɪzə bleɪd/
real (adj) /rɪəl/
smile (v) /smaɪl/
superb (adj) /su:'pɜ:b/
total (n) /'təʊtl/
unkind (adj) /ˌʌn'kaɪnd/
unluckily (adv) /ʌn'lʌkɪli/
unpleasant (adj) /ʌn'plezənt/
wave (v) /weɪv/
weather forecast (n) /'weðə 'fɔ:kɑ:st/
youth (n) /ju:θ/

UNIT 17

ban (v) /bæn/
calendar (n) /'kælɪndə/
Christian (adj) /'krɪstʃən/
congratulations (n) /kənˌgrætʃə'leɪʃənz/
cook (n) /kʊk/
cow (n) /kaʊ/
driving test (n) /'draɪvɪŋ test/
faithful (adj) /'feɪθfəl/
festival (n) /'festɪvəl/
guest (n) /gest/
injured (adj) /'ɪndʒəd/
lamp (n) /læmp/
last (v) /lɑ:st/
lend (v) /lend/
live (adj) (**live** music) /laɪv/
monkey (n) /'mʌŋki/
non-alcoholic (adj) /ˌnɒn ˌælkə'hɒlɪk/
originally (adv) /ə'rɪdʒənəli/
rabbit (n) /'ræbɪt/
recorded (adj) /rɪ'kɔ:dɪd/
religious (adj) /rɪ'lɪdʒəs/
revolution (n) /ˌrevə'lu:ʃən/
sober (adj) /'səʊbə/
soft drink (n) /sɒft 'drɪŋk/

UNIT 18

back door (n) /ˌbæk 'dɔ:/
be off (v) (to **be off** work) /bi 'ɒf/
come round (v) (= visit) /kʌm 'raʊnd/
decorate (v) /'dekəreɪt/
dislike (v) /dɪs'laɪk/
drums (n) /drʌmz/
dust (v) /dʌst/
hoover (v) /'hu:və/
iron (v) /'aɪən/
rubbish (n) /'rʌbɪʃ/
shopping (n) /'ʃɒpɪŋ/
sip (v) /sɪp/
teabag (n) /'ti:bæg/
tidy up (v) /ˌtaɪdi 'ʌp/

UNIT 19

baseball (n) /'beɪsbɔ:l/
basketball (n) /'bɑ:skɪtbɔ:l/
beat (v) (Liverpool **beat** Chelsea) /bi:t/
boo (v) /bu:/
bounce (v) /baʊns/
cheat (n) /tʃi:t/
cheat (v) /tʃi:t/
crowd (n) /kraʊd/
disappear (n) /ˌdɪsə'pɪə/
drop (v) /drɒp/
jogging (n) /'dʒɒgɪŋ/
kick (v) /kɪk/
be mad about (v) (= be very keen on)
    /bi'mæd ə'baʊt/
message (n) /'mesɪdʒ/
nun (n) /nʌn/
passion (n) /'pæʃən/
poor (n) (the **poor**) /pʊə/
prayer (n) /preə/
punch (v) /pʌntʃ/
recently (adv) /'ri:səntli/
reporter (n) /rɪ'pɔ:tə/
score (v) (to **score** a goal) /skɔ:/
share (v) /ʃeə/
squash (n) (to play **squash**) /skwɒʃ/
swimming costume (n) /'swɪmɪŋ
    ˌkɒstjʊm/
swimming pool (n) /'swɪmɪŋ pu:l/
team (n) /ti:m/
tennis court (n) /'tenɪs kɔ:t/
tennis racket (n) /'tenɪs ˌrækɪt/
win (v) /wɪn/
windsurfing (n) /'wɪnd ˌsɜ:fɪŋ/

UNIT 20

atmosphere (n) /'ætməsfɪə/
central heating (n) /ˌsentrəl 'hi:tɪŋ/
cocktail bar (n) /'kɒkteɪl bɑ:/
daily routine (n) /ˌdeɪli ru:'ti:n/
en-suite toilet (n) /ˌɒn 'swi:t 'tɔɪlət/
flame (n) /fleɪm/
nearby (adv) /ˌnɪə'baɪ/
power (n) (= electricity) /'paʊə/
receptionist (n) /rɪ'sepʃənɪst/
residential area (n) /ˌrezɪ'denʃəl 'eəriə/
smell (v) /smel/
traffic jam (n) /'træfɪk dʒæm/
unpack (v) /ʌn'pæk/

Tapescripts

Unit 1

RECORDING 5

INTERVIEWER: Hi, I hope it's OK if I record what you're saying on my tape-recorder. Then I can write it up for the magazine later.

ACTOR: That's fine. What do you want to ask me?

I: Well, all the newspapers are talking about your new film *Family Trouble*. Tell us something about it.

A: Well it's a comedy about a man who gets married too young and then has to make a choice between his family and his career.

I: And ... um are you married?

A: No, I'm too young to be married, don't you think?

I: How old are you? 22?

A: Yes, that's right.

I: But you do have a girlfriend at the moment.

A: Yes, I do. Her name is Isabelle. She plays my fiancée in *Family Trouble*. We have no plans to get married.

I: Do you live with her?

A: No, I live with my family in Los Angeles – my mum and dad and three sisters.

I: You are American, then?

A: Yes, I was born here in Britain but I am an American citizen.

I: What kind of music do you like?

A: Oh, all kinds. Classical, rock, rap. Jazz is my favourite, I guess.

I: I notice you always seem to wear black clothes. Is this your favourite colour?

A: No, not really. I mean I wear blue jeans and white T-shirts a lot. I don't like bright colours like red and yellow – that's true.

I: And, very important – your next film. Is it true that you're in a horror movie?

A: Yeah, *A Night with Frankenstein* ... it's about this guy...

Unit 2

RECORDING 2

INTERVIEWER: What do you spend your money on when you have it, Tanya?

TANYA: Oh, holidays. I don't spend anything for months. I just save and save, then, when I have enough, I go off for a week or two or longer – somewhere I've never been before or just somewhere warm to relax. And when I'm not on holiday I spend money on books.

I: Travel books?

T: Yes, well, all kinds of books, really.

I: David, what about you?

DAVID: Well, I'm a student, as you know, so I haven't got much money, unfortunately. What I have goes on music – CDs, mostly.

I: What kind of music?

D: Everything – classical, jazz, pop. I also like going to pop concerts, but they cost a lot, so, you know 'cos the tickets are so expensive. I also love clothes so if there's a sale, I buy casual things – jeans, shirts, jackets – that sort of thing.

RECORDING 3

INTERVIEWER: What kind of souvenirs do you bring back from your travels, Tanya?

TANYA: I usually buy something for the house or garden – you know, wooden parrots, big plant pots for my garden, small rugs. But it can be very difficult to bring souvenirs back. I once sat on a fifteen hour flight with an enormous plant pot on my knee – so big I couldn't see over the top. Then at the airport I put it down for a second and somebody fell over it and broke it!

I: Oh no!

T: I wasn't very pleased! I also love jewellery so – for example, in South America I bought lots of earrings and big necklaces.

I: And you, David?

DAVID: Well, music of course and also whatever's cheap – clothes in the States are cheap, for example. I collect T-shirts.

I: Really? How many have you got?

D: Oh, I've got about forty of them from all over the world. But you have to be careful – I remember one holiday I spent a long time deciding which T-shirt to buy and when I got back home they had exactly the same one in our local shop!

Unit 3

RECORDING 1

LUCY: So this is me standing between my parents, just after my wedding. (All right, yeah.) Mum and Dad are divorced, actually, but they still get on well. My Mum got married again last year and I did invite Philip – my stepfather – but he decided not to come. Then next to Mum there's my sister, Sarah – she's holding her new baby, Claudia, (Oh, that's nice.) and next to Dad is my brother-in-law, Ken. He's standing behind Ben – Ben's three. Behind them there's my brother Max. He's wearing that hat because he's an actor and likes to look different. (Oh, right.) My older brother Tom couldn't come because he's working in Brazil at the moment – he's an engineer. He's engaged and they're getting married at Christmas. Um... anyway, on Max's right are Granny and Grandad – they're in their eighties now (They look great.) – and they adore Max – he's definitely the favourite. Nana – Mum's Mum – is on the other side. Then at the back are my uncle, my aunts and cousins: Mum's sister, Auntie Gill, with Uncle Rob – he's Australian, actually, and their twins, Harry and Sam – they're twenty-five. (They look alike, don't they?) Yeah. Aunt Pat is my Dad's sister. She's just separated from her husband, which I'm glad about, because I can't stand him so he didn't come. Anyway, so that's all my relations.

RECORDING 6

TOM: My Grandad always spends his money on other people, not on himself – you know, even if he hasn't got much money he'll buy you what you want for your birthday. And he's never bad-tempered – he always smiles and says nice things. And what I like about my Mum – she waits for ages for my little brother to get ready and tells him the same things lots of times but doesn't lose her temper.

DIANA: The cat's the best person in our family. She always comes and jumps on you and licks you and is really loving. She loves playing – she really seems to enjoy life. The next best is my Dad – he always says what he thinks – he can't tell a lie. If he does, he goes red. I like that.

Unit 4

RECORDING 1

1 MAN: Good morning. The Bistro, Fulham Road.
EMMA: Hello. Is there a table free on Thursday evening, please, at about eight o'clock? For six people.
M: So that's the eighteenth of August, isn't it? I'll just check. I'm afraid there isn't one free until eight forty-five. Is that too late?
E: No, that's OK.
M: Could I take your name, please?
E: Yes, it's Emma Matthews. That's M-A- double T-H-E-W-S.
M: And may I have your phone number?
E: Of course. It's five four three, one double two.

2 CAROL: Hello, seven one three, four double seven.
EMMA: Hello. Is that Carol? This is Emma.
C: Hi there. Do you want to speak to Simon?
E: Is he in?
C: I think so. Hang on a minute.
SIMON: Hi, Emma.
E: Hi, Simon. How are you? Listen. I think I can get a tennis court for Wednesday afternoon. Would you like to play?
S: Yeah, I'd love to. I've got a meeting that afternoon, but it should be over by five.
E: Shall I book it for five thirty then?
S: That would be fine.

3 RECEPTIONIST: Good morning. Gold Street surgery. How can I help you?
EMMA: Morning. I'd like to make an appointment for my daughter please, with Doctor Brown. For a check-up.
R: Right. When would you like the appointment?
E: Some time next week would be fine.
R: Can you hold, please?.... Would two twenty five next Tuesday be possible?
E: Oh... That's great. That's the twenty-third, isn't it?
R: Yes, and your daughter's name is ..?

RECORDING 4

SAM: Can we hire a car while we're there?
TRAVEL AGENT: Yes, you can, but remember to take your driving licence with you, won't you?
KAREN: What can we do in the evenings?
TA: Well, you can go to bars and restaurants to eat and dance. Or you can stay in the hotel. There's usually a show there.
SAM: Do we have to get a visa for Romania?
TA: No, but you have to take your passports.

Unit 5

RECORDING 1

1 A: Thirty litres, please. Four star.
   B: Shall I check your oil as well?

2 A: Do we have to get a ticket? It costs sixty p an hour.
   B: Yes, but there's a traffic warden over there and we don't want a fine!

3 A: The train now approaching platform one is the eleven oh five service to Manchester Oxford Street, calling at...

4 A: Last call for passengers flying to Barbados, flight BA two five five. Please report to Gate Number six immediately.

5 A: What's the fare to King Street, please?
   B: Twenty eight p please, sir.

RECORDING 3

NEWSREADER: And finally, a woman from Tewkesbury was left waiting for five hours in a car on the motorway yesterday while her forgetful husband went home without her!
   Thomas Brown and his wife Catherine were going to the seaside in their old car when it broke down. They were going on a day trip to Devon. They were travelling along the M5 at Clevedon, near Bristol, when the car broke down. So Mr Brown parked the car on the hard shoulder and went off to find help. His wife knew this would take time as the seventy-three-year-old man walked with two sticks. But she didn't realise just how long!
   Five hours later the police found Mrs Brown, eighty-four, still in the car on the hard shoulder on the M5! Mr Brown was already at home in Tewkesbury! When he left his wife in the car, he took a bus to Bristol and then a train home to Tewkesbury – a seventy mile journey.
   'I suppose I forgot,' Mr Brown said. 'I was very surprised when the police arrived at home.'

RECORDING 5

MUM: You have remembered it's Dad's birthday on Monday, haven't you?
TESS: Yes, but I really don't know what to get him. He's got everything!
MAX: Well, I've already decided on my present. I saw it in a shop in town. I'm going to get him a video about playing golf.
T: Oh. What about you, Mum?
M: I'm not actually buying him a present. I'm taking him to London for the evening. I've booked a table at a new Italian restaurant I've heard about and then we're going to the theatre. I got the tickets last week but he doesn't know. It's a surprise.
T: Oh, that's an idea! I think I'll buy him something nice to wear then. A new tie or something. What...?

RECORDING 7

Tomorrow

I'd really like to get up early,
I think I'll jog to work,
I'm going to cycle and swim and run,
I'm giving up chips, of course,
Or am I? On second thoughts,
Maybe I'll wait until the day after tomorrow.

Unit 7

RECORDING 4

INTERVIEWER: What's it like being a teenager these days? Do you worry about what's happening in the world?

CHRIS: Well, I watch the news and so on but I don't really care about politics – I don't think about it that much. I
5 do worry about the environment, though – it seems to be getting worse and worse all the time.

PENNY: So do I. These days it's even dangerous to go out in the sun. I worry about animals, too, and how they're treated – that's why I'm a vegetarian. My Dad is fed up
10 with me not eating meat – he likes the typical meat and two veg – and he hopes I'll change my mind and start eating meat again, but I won't.

C: But really it's everyday things that worry kids of our age, you know, how to get on with your parents and so
15 on.

I: Do you argue with them?

C: Well, we argue about clothes because they like me to wear smart clothes and I like old ripped jeans. But I usually wear what I want in the end. It's important to me
20 to look good and be in fashion.

P: I wear jeans or go to second-hand shops for my clothes. You can get really cheap clothes there which are nearly new. But I do care about what my parents think of me. My Mum doesn't mind if I dye my hair – I dyed it
25 red last week and she said it looked nice – but she wouldn't let me wear a ring in my nose.

C: We argue about housework, too. I hate it and they're always telling me to do the washing up.

I: Do they stop you doing anything?

30 P: Well, I can only go out at the weekend. My Dad usually picks me up in the car at eleven and I feel stupid in front of my friends. Young people have to learn to be independent and try different things. A lot of the young people at my school smoke, for example, but their
35 parents don't know. I have smoked but I gave up. A lot of the boys drink, too. I think it's better if parents just let them do it – not encourage them but not stop them either.

I: So what about the future?

40 P: Well, I'm going to art college in the autumn.

C: Maybe I'll get married, probably at twenty-eight and I'll have two kids. I'd like to be rich. I don't want to live in Britain, because there's not much work and it's cold and boring.

Unit 8

RECORDING 2

IRENE: I'm not nervous when I'm out by myself in the dark. When our two boys were little I took them with me. They loved it. It seems to have given them a healthy life and both of them are milkmen now. I sing as I go along the quiet empty streets. I like hymns and Elvis Presley. I love the night. You see some wonderful things, like ducks going in a line down the main road. There are hedgehogs and squirrels, too.

Everything is so peaceful and still. You see a few people, policemen, nightworkers and so on but sometimes you're all alone. I think a lot while I'm out – usually about the past.

I haven't had a day off in eleven years. I'm never ill – it's all the milk I drink! Even when we went to London to get the award we got up at two in the morning to deliver the milk before we went.

RECORDING 4

ANDREW: I've decided to sell my house and give up my job because I want to do something different. I'd like to study how the gorillas live and then I hope to write a book about it. Maybe some people think I'm mad but I really feel I just need to do something useful with my life.

INTERVIEWER: What about living in difficult conditions? How do you feel about that?

A: I don't mind living in difficult conditions – that's no problem. The only thing is I'll miss seeing my friends. I've promised to write to them every week and tell them about it.

Unit 9

RECORDING 1

1 ESTATE AGENT: Are you looking for a fairly big place?

WOMAN: Well, no, now we've retired we don't need so much space – but John's leg's bad so we'd prefer to have a bungalow. We'd like to live in the country or by the sea, and we need a spare bedroom for when our son comes to stay.

2 ESTATE AGENT: So you are looking for a house with what – about three bedrooms?

MAN: Yes, it must have three bedrooms and also a garden for the dog. Otherwise the only important thing is to be quite near schools, for the kids, and shops and so on.

ESTATE AGENT: And are you looking for an old house, or a modern one?

MAN: We'd rather have an old detached house but we haven't got enough money so we'll have to go for a semi, I suppose.

3 ESTATE AGENT: How can I help you?

YOUNG WOMAN: I'm looking for somewhere cheap to live while I'm at college. I don't care too much, because I'll sell it when I leave. Something in the centre of town, with a modern kitchen.

Unit 10

RECORDING 1

Group A

MAN: Yes, it's true British people seem more relaxed – in public, anyway. For instance, if a train is late with no explanation, people don't complain or get angry, they just carry on reading their newspapers. But it's not because they're relaxed – they're probably furious inside. It's because they hate showing their feelings – they hate people looking at them. If a small child is screaming in a supermarket, for example, the mother looks embarrassed – you shouldn't show your feelings in public! I do agree about the sense of humour. British people love playing with words – they can be very funny, and they can tell a joke without laughing – they can keep a completely straight face. I don't agree that people are polite though – maybe in small towns, but not in big cities like London. Drivers and shop assistants can be very rude.

RECORDING 2

Group B

WOMAN: Yes, when I'm away from Britain I miss the people because they're so unconventional – they're all different. You can see it in the way they dress – young people don't follow fashion. They're all individuals. I'm sure that's why there are so many different accents and cultures all over Britain, too – people don't like being the same. Yes, I think in general people are kind. In a village post office they will probably take the time to ask a little old lady, 'How's your knee?' And they are always ready to help and give money if there is a disaster and also to Oxfam and other charities – especially animal charities like the RSPCA! They can seem unfriendly, or a bit cold at first, to people they don't know, but they're not really. A lot of British people are very friendly indeed.

Unit 11

RECORDING 2

PHILIP: Sarah and I don't spend our free time doing crosswords. We lead a very active life. When we're not working we enjoy rock-climbing or parachuting or going on safari in Africa. I've even learnt how to fly a plane. I suppose our favourite pastime though is deep-sea diving. Especially in the Caribbean. I remember once we took the boat into the Gulf of Mexico. The water wasn't very clear. We all went in except Jules. He stayed on the boat. There were some fantastic sights. Amazing creatures I'd never seen before. It was magic with the light on. A kind of wonderland. It wasn't very deep and we were near the bottom. Then all of a sudden I saw Sarah waving her arms at me. She looked frantic. I didn't realise what it was at first. I thought she couldn't breathe or something. Then I saw it. This incredible great shark coming towards me. I've never moved so fast in my life. Luckily, it wasn't interested in me. It just went straight past. Perhaps it wasn't a man-eater or it was short-sighted or something.

Unit 12

RECORDING 1

1 A: Nice to see you again.
  B: Hi! How are you? I hear you've not been very well.
  A: I'm fine now, thanks. How about you?

2 A: Hello, Sally.
  B: Hello. Thanks very much for Tom's present. It was just what he wanted.
  A: You're welcome.

3 A: Is Colin here?
  B: Colin who?
  A: You know. Colin Wilson. I want to see him.
  A: I don't think so. I haven't seen him.

4 A: It's a bit chilly today, isn't it?
  B: Yes, I think it's going to snow.
  A: I hope not. We're playing football later.

RECORDING 2

1 ANNOUNCER: Last night in Windsor a burglar broke into a house and stole a mobile phone. Later he rang the owner offering to sell it half-price for two hundred pounds...

2 Yesterday morning at Burnham a robber tied up a bank manager and took thousands of pounds. The bank manager dialled nine, nine, nine with his tongue and called the police. The police later arrested the robber.

3 A thief walked into an electrical shop in Hitchin and loaded a washing machine into his car. He calmly drove away. The man has been sent to prison for six months.

Unit 13

RECORDING 1

PENNY: Now listen carefully. When you come out of the station on to Waverley Bridge, turn right and go straight on until you get to Princes Street. Turn left and walk along Princes Street for about fifteen minutes. Go past the Royal Scottish Academy. You'll see the Castle and the Mound on your left. When you get to the end of Princes Street (you'll see the Caledonian Hotel in front of you), turn left again into Lothian Road. Walk straight along Lothian Road and after five minutes you'll see the Usher Hall on your left, opposite the Sheraton Hotel.

RECORDING 2

I feel it in my fingers
I feel it in my toes
Well, love is all around me
and so the feeling grows.
It's written on the wind,
It's everywhere I go.
So if you really love me
Come on and let it show.

RECORDING 3 (As Recording 2)

You know I love you,
I always will.
My mind's made up
By the way that I feel.
There's no beginning, there'll be no end
'Cos on my love, you can depend.

I see your face before me,
As I lay on my bed.
I kind of get to thinking,
Of all the things you said.
You gave your promise to me,
And I gave mine to you.
I need someone beside me,
In everything I do.

It's written on the wind
It's everywhere I go.
So if you really love me
Come on and let it show.

RECORDING 4

1 A: I met him last night. He works here. He's nearly bald and rather short.
  B: We have a lot of people here like that, sir.
  A: Well, he's got a round face with a pointed nose.
  B: I see.
  A: And a beard.
  B: Well, that could be Mr Page...

2 A: Yes, she's in her mid-twenties and really slim.
  POLICEWOMAN: Fine. Can you give me more details? What colour are her eyes?
  A: Let me see. Yes, she's got large green eyes.
  P: Yes, yes I'm sure. You say she's missing.
  A: Yes, she didn't come home...

3 A: Excuse me, I'm looking for my girlfriend.
  B: Oh, dear! Have you lost her?
  A: Yes, she's... eh... average height, not pretty... quite plain in fact... and a... eh... bit overweight I suppose.
  B: That's not a very nice way to talk about your girlfriend!
  A: Sorry... I mean... No... Let me think. She's got short curly hair with a square face, green eyes.
  B: I think I know who you mean. She was the person I saw getting on a plane for Paris with a very good-looking, wonderfully handsome man who looked like a film star...
  A: What?!

4 A: Excuse me. I'm looking for a friend of mine. I said I'd meet him here.
  B: What does he look like?
  A: Um... He's quite tall and well-built. And he's got long black hair. Oh yes, and he's got a beard and he wears glasses.
  B: Oh, him. Yes. He's in the lounge...

Unit 14

RECORDING 4

NIKKI: We're not going out tonight, are we?
TOM: No, let's not. I'm too tired. Let's see what's on TV.
N: Well, there's 'Star Trek' at 6.30. I'm a fan of William Shatner. He's a good actor, isn't he?
T: I don't like him very much. Let me have a look. 'Headhunters'. That sounds interesting.
N: I can't stand Francesca Annis.
T: Well, I want to watch it.
N: OK, we'll watch it if I can watch 'Star Trek'.
T: 'Panorama' doesn't sound very interesting this week.
N: And it wasn't very good last week, was it?
T: No. Let's see what else there is. You still like Sting, don't you? He's on.
N: Yes. I certainly want to watch him.
T: I think this wildlife programme's been on before. The one about the elephants. We've seen it, haven't we?
N: Yes, we have. I don't want to see that again.
T: What about Rory Bremner? You liked him last time, didn't you?
N: All right.
T: Yes, let's watch that, shall we?

Unit 15

RECORDING 2

KAREN: Well, the day starts at eight o'clock. You stop for lunch at twelve and then you leave school in the middle of the afternoon. Then you go home or do some sport.
RIE: School starts at half-past eight and we have to be there at about eight o'clock. It finishes at four o'clock in the afternoon but we have many different activities so we have to stay at school until seven o'clock every evening.

RECORDING 3

Group A

KAREN: We don't have very many rules at our school back in the States. The main rules are: no drugs, no smoking and no fighting, but there are crazy rules too like no wearing hats.
INTERVIEWER: What happens if someone breaks the rules?
K: Then you have to stay in the classroom at lunchtime which is crazy because you just spend your time talking to your friends. If you do something serious, like drugs, they call the cops.
I: Do you have to wear a uniform?
K: No, you can wear what you want but everybody wants to wear the latest fashions, which is crazy in school.
I: And are the teachers very strict?
K: No, not really. You can do what you want in class, talk in class, even when the teachers are talking. They don't really mind.
I: How does your school in America compare with your school in Britain?
K: In the States, you can do what you want when you want. You can miss classes – they don't really care – but here in England it's very strict and you have a lot more rules, a uniform and things like that.

RECORDING 4

Group B

INTERVIEWER: Are there many rules in your school in Japan?

RIE: Yes, a lot. For example, we have to wear a school uniform but we mustn't go to town in a uniform. We have to go home first and change into our normal clothes.

I: What's the uniform like?

R: The traditional Japanese school uniform is navy blue with a long skirt. Sometimes it's quite pretty, but no one likes it. The modern uniform with a short skirt is quite popular.

I: Do you have to work hard in your school?

R: Yes, very. And our teachers are very strict. If we don't study hard they punish us.

I: What kind of punishments do they give you?

R: We have to stay late after school and study. Sometimes the teachers phone our parents and our parents have to come to school.

I: Rie, how does your school in Japan compare with your school in Britain?

R: My school in Japan is a girls' school but here it is a mixed school. In Japan we have fifty students in one class and we stay in the same room all day. Here there are only twenty students and we have to move each lesson.

Unit 16

RECORDING 2

ANDREW: You didn't ring me last night.

NICOLA: Sorry?

A: I said you didn't ring me last night.

N: I know. I went back to work.

A: What was the problem?

PASSENGER: Sorry.

N: Oh, sorry. Are you trying to get off?

P: Yes.

N: I had to phone America.

A: Oh yes?

N: Yes. I had to talk to our American director. Why don't we meet tonight?

A: No, I don't think so.

N: Oh, damn! Why won't this work?

OFFICIAL: Can I have a look at your ticket? Sorry but this is out of date. Would you come with me?

N: Oh, no. Did I forget to buy a ticket?

Unit 17

RECORDING 1

1 A: Put this present under the tree.
  B: Oh, thanks!
  A: You mustn't open it until the morning.
  B: OK.
  A: And don't eat too much tomorrow.
  B: Impossible! I always do.

2 A: I want to see the fireworks.
  B: Oh, I'll come with you.
  C: Have a good time, you two! And be careful! Don't get too near the bonfire.

3 A: Have you made your resolutions yet?
  B: Yes, I'm going to give up smoking.
  A: What, again?!

4 A: Oh, what a horrible sight! Here take these sweets.
  B: Thanks very much. Thank you.
  A: Not at all. Now go away!

5 A: Darling.
  B: Yes?
  A: Who was that card from?
  B: I don't know. There's no name on it.
  H: You went very red when the postman came.
  W: Did I?
  H: Yes. It's not from your new boss, is it?

Unit 18

RECORDING 1

1 A: Are you all right?
  B: Oh, could you give me a hand with these, please?
  A: Sure. Where do you want them?
  B: I'm trying to get them to my car.
  A: OK.

2 A: I'm going into town. Shall I post those for you?
  B: No thanks, I'm not quite ready yet. Oh, but can you get me some stamps, please?
  A: Sure.

3 A: Damn! I need two fifty ps. I'm sorry to trouble you but have you got any change?
  B: I don't know. Let me have a look. Sorry. No. I've only got a five pound note.

4 A: Tom. Excuse me. Could you give me a push?
  B: Sorry?
  A: I said do you think you could give me a push?
  B: OK.

5 HUSBAND: Hello. Oh, little Oscar.
  NEIGHBOUR: Hello.
  WIFE: I hear you're going away.
  N: Yes, I am. Would you mind looking after Oscar for a few days?
  W: Ah! I'm afraid we're going away too. Sorry.

RECORDING 2

Group A

HENRY: The music's so loud – thump, thump, thump, nearly every night. It gives me headaches and I have to lie down. I've been off work because of the noise. You can't imagine having a headache and hearing that noise. Sometimes I get really angry. The other night I went into the garden and shouted 'Shut up'. I phoned the police but they said they couldn't do anything. A lot of young people come and go. Sometimes they come into my garden and move my pot plants. Or knock on my front door. I don't mind if they have a good time but there has to be a limit. If they're going to have a party, at least they could tell me and I'd go out. It used to be very quiet round here.

RECORDING 3

Group B

TIM: It's sad that we are annoying this man next door. We had no idea. Sure we like music in the day and we sometimes have loud parties. But we've never had any trouble. If anyone wants to complain they can always come round. We're not going to get into a fight. I play loud music to wake myself up. About ten in the morning that's when it's the loudest. Yes, another person here plays very loud music but not all the time. Me I play music quietly when I'm up. I haven't had a party for six months. I'm surprised Mr Skitt is bothered. Perhaps he doesn't like the kind of music. Heavy metal or rap. I hear Mr Skitt's TV all the time and I hear him shouting at his cats but that's what you get if you live close to people. We obviously have a different way of life. I play the drums but I try not to be too loud. That's why I play them in the cellar.

Unit 19

RECORDING 1

1 ZOE: In a formal situation you should shake hands and say 'Nice to meet you' or 'How do you do.' We don't usually kiss people when we first meet them.

2 Always order at the bar. Take your drinks and sit down where you can find a seat. Here people sometimes share a table. To get food you usually order at the bar, too. There aren't usually any waiters although sometimes they will bring you your food.

3 Don't forget to ask before you have a bath or a shower. And try not to spend too long in the bathroom!

4 Never clap your hands or hit your glass with a knife. Say 'Excuse me!' or try to catch the waiter's eye.

5 People normally expect you to be a few minutes late. Never arrive early. Usually you have drinks before the meal. After you eat, you usually sit around chatting for a while. If you want to leave soon after the meal make sure you say you've had a lovely evening and the food was delicious and then make an excuse.

RECORDING 2

FATHER: What are you going to do when you get there?
TIM: I'll go straight to the hotel. I'll probably be very tired.
M: How will we know that you're all right?
T: Oh, Mum. Don't worry. I'll call you as soon as I can.
F: Then make sure you phone your uncle. Have you got your traveller's cheques?
T: Yes, Dad.
M: What will you do if he's not there when you phone? He won't know you're at the hotel.
T: I'll try again later. It'll be OK.
F: He won't come and pick you up unless you phone.
T: I know. Please don't worry.
M: Have you got everything? Have you packed your woollen socks and your big jumper?
T: Yes.
M: And your uncle's present. Don't forget. Give it to him as soon as you see him.
T: Yes.

Unit 20

RECORDING 2

ANNOUNCER: According to the latest survey the British still like their holidays. These are the results. 90% enjoy the beauties of nature and the countryside and 89% like being away from home and the daily routine. The same number – 89% like spending more time with the family and friends. This was surprising. In fact, according to the survey, family holidays seem to be good for family relationships. These are the other figures about what the British like. 88% of the British people we asked, like meeting new people and 87% like seeing life in different countries. A lot of people think the British don't like meeting new people but according to this survey this is not true. New kinds of food interested 79% of the people and 60% were mainly interested in lying on the beach and getting a suntan. Most people admit to putting on weight on holiday. Going to museums and art galleries interested only 58% and even fewer – a surprising 35% – just like drinking a lot. On the other hand, what people most dislike about their holidays is the journey. In particular not having information about why they have been delayed – 76% – while 72% hate any kind of waiting at the airport. The same number – 72% – hate traffic jams. The journey is often the most difficult part of the holiday. These are the other figures about what the British dislike. 58% of people hate paying too much for something and 56% hate noisy or rude people. However, 46% of the people we asked, complain about getting lost and arguing with each other and 37% say they hate fighting to get a place by the swimming pool. At the bottom of the list only 32% worry about not speaking the language – we think this would be different for other nationalities – and 27% hate packing. The survey suggests that the British like being with other people than we think. Interestingly, more than a quarter arrive home as tired as or more tired than when they went.

Acknowledgements

We are grateful to the following for permission to reproduce copyright material:

The authors, Tessa Boase & Tom Hodgkinson for an extract from their article 'I'm a Real Fan' in *The Daily Telegraph* 19.11.93; the Author's Agent for the adapted article 'How to eat spaghetti' by Antonio Carluccio in *Daily Mail* 30.10.93 © 1993; the Author's Agent for adapted extracts from *George's Marvellous Medicine* by Roald Dahl (publ. Jonathan Cape Ltd & Penguin Books Ltd); Ewan Macnaughton Associates for the adapted article 'Light Snack' in *The Daily Telegraph* 17.07.93; EMAP Woman's Group Ltd for an adapted extract from the article 'Want to be together forever?' in *New Woman* February, 1994; The Guardian for adapted extracts from the articles 'A Corner of Japan forever Cotswold' by Michael Prestage in *The Guardian* © 19.04.94, and 'Urban myths: call me mother' by Healey & Glanvill in *The Guardian Weekend* © 30.10.93; The National Magazine Company Ltd for an adapted extract from the article 'Postcards from the Edge' in *Good Housekeeping* magazine, September 1992 © National Magazine Company; Newspaper Publishing plc for adapted extracts from the articles 'She delivers kindness with the pintas' by Susan de Muth in *The Independent* 8.12.93, 'Daily bread' by Deborah Bull in *The Independent on Sunday* 14.11.93, and 'Barbra and her funny girl fans' by David Lester in *The Independent on Sunday* 10.04.94; Polygram International Music Publishing Ltd for the lyrics 'Love is All Around' written by Reg Presley © 1967 Dick James Music Ltd; Solo Syndication Ltd for adapted extracts from the articles ' A Lion with roar energy' by Graham Bridgstock in *Evening Standard* 18.01.94, 'Should we ever ask a police-woman to play seductress just to win a case?' by Geoffrey Levy in *Daily Mail* 12.03.94, 'Age of consent' by Marina Cantacuzino in Daily Mail 18.02.93, 'Inside story Carol Thatcher' by Clare Campbell in *Daily Mail* Weekend 22.1.94 and 'Wing and a Prayer' by Simon Kinnersley in *Mail on Sunday* 06.03.94; The Observer for an adaptation of the questionnaire 'Are You a Workaholic', p58 in the *Observer Colour Supplement* © The Observer; the author, David Thomas for an adapted extract from his article 'Nick and Kate Moss' in *The Daily Telegraph* 15.10.93.

We have unfortunately been unable to trace the copyright holder of the article 'Healthstyle Extra: Paul Smith' in *The Sunday Express Magazine* October 1989 and would appreciate any information which would enable us to do so.

We are grateful to the following for permission to reproduce copyright photographs:

Ace Photo Agency/Crysse Morrison for page 102MR; Allsport (UK) Ltd for page 115T; Alton Towers for page 48B; Austine J. Brown/Aviation Picture Library for page 48T; The Bridgeman Art Library/©D.A.C.S for page 42(a); Camera Press Ltd/Denzil McNeelance for page 19L & R, /Richard Open for page 25(A); J Allan Cash Ltd for page 54(1), 109(main); Comstock Photolibrary for page 91L; Greg Evans Photolibrary for page 12(a & d), 50TR, 54(3); Tim Graham-London for page 15; The Ronald Grant Archive for page 79; Robert Harding Picture Library for page 30(b & c), 34(b), 68(h), 54(2), 60M, /Martyn F. Chillmaid for page 43TM, /Ian Griffiths for page 34(d), /Adam Woolfitt for page 12(c), 43TR; Hulton Deutsch for page 29TL & B, 60B, /David Eason for page 29TR; The Image Bank for page 102ML, /Alan Becker for page 12(b), /G. Coliva for page 13(inset), /Joe Devenney for page 102TL, /Romilly Lockyer for page 102TR, /G & M David De Lossy for page 91L(inset); The Independant/Geraint Lewis for page 85(B), /Susan de Muth for page 49; Ink Group Publishers for page 16; Katz Pictures ©1992 for page 86; The Kobal Collection for page 6T & M, 117(inset); ©Longman Group/Gareth Boden for page 14, 24, 36, 40T & (a-c), 42TL, 75R, 88, 92, 93L, 96(a & b), 102BR, 109(inset), /Trevor Clifford for page 10(c & e), 18, 30(d & e), 40(d), 42(b & c), 45, 75L, 118, 125; ©Lufthansa for page 10(b); Mail Newspapers/Solo Syndication for page 56, 115M; Mirror Syndication for page 78; The Moviestore Collection for page 6B, 117T; M.O.M.I for page 48LM; PhotoBank for page 91R; Press Association/Rebecca Naden for page 102BL(inset); Retna Pictures/John Atashian for page 85T, /Onyx for page 87; Rex Features Ltd for page 7, 25(B), 37, /Brooker for page 60T; The Royal Ballet/Anthony Crickman for page 40B; ©Bill Sanderson for page 61; Tony Stone Images for page 68(f), /Andy Cox for page 43TL, /Tony Craddock for page 10(a), /Dale Durfee for page 17(1), /David H. Endersbee for page 102BL, /Ken Fisher for page 17(2), /John Garrett for page 10(d), /Janet Gill for page 120, /Chris Harver for page 68(c), /Stephen Krasemann, /Tom Parker for page 54(4), /Manoj Shah for page 68(d & g), /Hugh Sitton for page 34(e), /Art Wolfe for page 50TL; Telegraph Colour Library for page 13(main), 34(a), 93R, /Bavaria Bildagentur for page 34(c), /M. Krasowitz for page 91R(inset), /Dia Max for page 30(a), /Planet Earth/Steve Bloom for page 68(e), Planet Earth/Linda Pitkin for page 48UM, Planet Earth/Jonathan Scott for page 68(a), /Tom Wilson for page 26.

Illustrated by

1-11 Line Art (Maps), Kathy Baxendale (h/w), Julia Bigg (The Inkshed), Paul Davies (Garden Studio), Stephen Dell, Andrew Farmer (Edinburgh map), Ramsay Gibb (Beint & Beint), Michael A Hill, Rod Holt, Lorna Kent, Harry North, Panteus Palios, Eric Smith, Graham Thompson, Lis Watkins (Pennant), Gary Wing, Allen Wittert (Pennant).

Cover illustration by Zap Art.